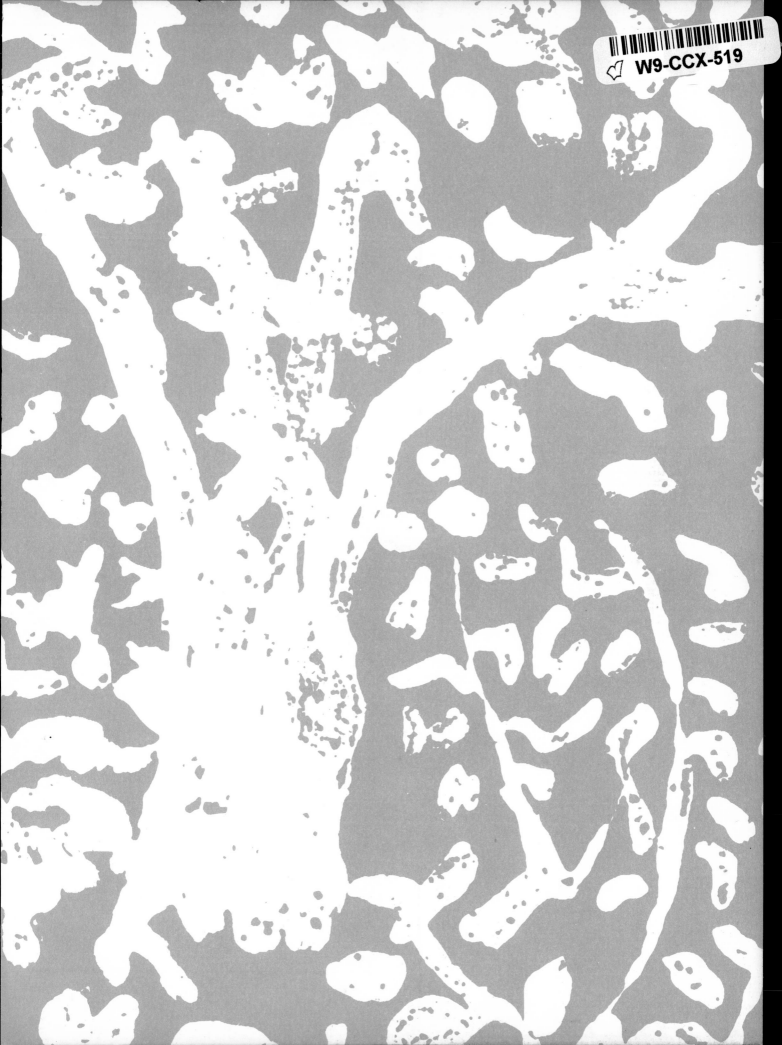

BILLY BALDWIN REMEMBERS

BILLY BALDWIN REMEMBERS

by Billy Baldwin

HᴚU

HARCOURT BRACE JOVANOVICH

New York and London

DESIGNED BY PHILIP GRUSHKIN

Printed in the United States of America

First edition

B   C   D   E

Library of Congress Cataloging in Publication Data
Baldwin, Billy.
    Billy Baldwin remembers.
    1. Baldwin, Billy. 2. Interior decorators—United States—Correspondence, reminiscences, etc.   I. Title.
NK2004.3.B34A22   747'.21'3   74-8712
ISBN 0-15-112070-6

The photographs on pages 57-61 (by Samuel Gottsche) are copyright © 1936, 1963 by The Condé Nast Publications Inc.; 64, 65, 68 (by Nyholm), copyright © 1939, 1967 by The Condé Nast Publications Inc.; 124, 125 (by Kertesz), copyright © 1946 by The Condé Nast Publications Inc.; 126 (by Kertesz), copyright © 1951 by The Condé Nast Publications Inc.; 127 (by Danny Wann), copyright © 1955 by The Condé Nast Publications Inc.; 128, 129 top (by Horst), copyright © 1965 by The Condé Nast Publications Inc.; 134 (by Horst), copyright © 1972 by The Condé Nast Publications Inc.; 149 (by Horst), copyright © 1965 by The Condé Nast Publications Inc.; 183 (by Norman Parkinson), copyright © 1969 by The Condé Nast Publications Inc.; 185 (by Horst), copyright © 1965 by The Condé Nast Publications Inc.; 204 (by Horst), copyright © 1974 by The Condé Nast Publications Inc.; 209 (by Beadle), copyright © 1970 by The Condé Nast Publications Inc.; 220, 221, 223, 224, 226-229 (by Horst), copyright © 1973 by The Condé Nast Publications Inc.; 148, 215-217, copyright © 1974 by Horst; 37 top, by Louise Dahl-Wolfe, is used by courtesy of Harper's Bazaar; 41, by courtesy of Madame Bernard Boutet de Monvel; 111, by courtesy of El Diario–La Prensa; 116, by permission of NBC News; 184, by courtesy of Tiffany & Co.; 187 top, by courtesy of Home Furnishings Daily; 208, by courtesy of The Metropolitan Museum of Art. The photographs on pages 15-20, 23-31, 97, 100, 103, 129 bottom, 130, 131, 137, 145, 146, 205 are by Horst; 37 bottom, 179, by Jerome Zerbe; 38, 143, by John Rawlings; 44, 45, 47, by Drix Duryea; 94, by Hans Mayr; 140 top right, 144, by Cecil Beaton. End papers are reproductions of "Foliage" by Woodson Wallpaper. The frontispiece is by Henry Koehler. The drawing on page 75 is by Charles Heileman, copyright © 1952 by The Condé Nast Publications Inc.; 183, by Richard DeMenocal, copyright © 1953 by The Condé Nast Publications Inc.; 185, copyright © 1947 by The Condé Nast Publications Inc. The floor plan on page 130 is by Brotman.

FOR WOODSON TAULBEE

CONTENTS

The author wishes to acknowledge the gracious help and co-operation of Miss Elizabeth Baer, of the Evergreen House Foundation, the invaluable assistance of Coralee Leon for editing the text and captions, and the continuing generosity of Horst for his photographs.

BILLY BALDWIN REMEMBERS

CHAPTER 1

Romance at Wye House: The Orangery, 1925

THE TIME WAS THE MID-1920's. I was fresh out of Princeton, where I had spent more time at New York parties, theatres, and museums than in front of my books. I was, like young men everywhere, full of grand ideas, and very impressionable.

One spring morning, my favorite aunt, at whose house on the Eastern Shore of Maryland I was visiting, hustled me into her car and announced that we were going to see Wye House, an old plantation near Easton.

Wye House, she told me, was built in 1661—more than a hundred years before the American Revolution—on a flat piece of land in Talbot County granted by the king to a Welshman named Edward Lloyd. It was plundered, abandoned, and rebuilt in the trying years of the early 1770's, but after three hundred years and considerable diminishment in acreage it was still in the possession of the Lloyd family. Almost every one of Wye's owners had been named Edward, which made its history somewhat confusing. What is clear is that the Lloyds of Talbot County had been a powerful influence on the young nation: nearly all of them had been deeply involved in government.

My aunt's stories excited me. The Lloyds had a reputation for hospitality that extended all the way back to Wales, and I began to envision life as it might have been on a large Maryland plantation: the great parties on the bowling green in summer, and, in winter, the idle evenings by the fire with friends all laughing and etching their names into the parlor windows with the diamonds in their stickpins and brooches (the diamond-writing is clearly visible today). Then she said there was the orangery, a brick and glass house built to protect the orange and other citrus trees from the winter cold.

The orangery at Wye was one of only two built in the eighteenth century in America, and was so celebrated that a man once rode eighteen miles on horseback in the middle of winter so that he might have a single lemon—and then wrote the Lloyds a letter of praise and thanks.

By the time we reached Wye House, I had become very curious.

"Wye is full of surprises," my aunt said, smiling, "that one must discover for oneself. I will be back in due time." And off she drove.

I was alone. The vast property—still more than a thousand acres—stretched before me. Below a sunk fence (we called them ha-ha walls because animals thought they could be jumped over) beyond the entrance gates, a herd of black-legged Suffolk sheep was grazing. Ahead of me spread the gardens: well-kept shrubs of gardenias, camellias, crape myrtles, and all kinds of fruit trees. Back of the house there was an intricate boxwood maze, which proved to be almost impenetrable.

I walked on through a small forest where birds twittered busily at one another. There, hidden among trees, I came across a great pair of brick gateposts topped by stone baskets of fruit. Stepping through, I found myself in a little family graveyard, very peaceful and romantic, quite without any chilly associations. Some of the headstones were beautiful obelisks; others stone slabs like beds or tables, held above the ground by stout sculptured legs. After a time, I stepped back through the gates and circled around the wood to the path that led to the house.

Wye House itself is a large, plain frame building painted white and dark green, at once very modest and very proud, like all the great eighteenth-century American houses I know so well. As I drew near I saw, at the distant end of the broad bowling green, the Orangery.

I felt a sudden shock of beauty so strong that I could only stand frozen in wonder. There amid all this Americana stood a lovely building as French as the Trianon of Versailles. It was in the style of Louis XVI, a fantastic contrast to the English Georgian houses I was accustomed to seeing in my home state. The orangery was of white-painted brick, with enormous tall windows composed of hundreds of tiny square panes of glass designed to admit the warmth and light of the sun. Ivy twined up its walls, and beside it, bordering the bowling green, were ancient fragrant lilacs now in full bloom.

No beautiful building before or since has affected me as profoundly as the Orangery, perhaps because it was so unexpected. As I stood entranced, there emerged from a window a splendid peacock, who proceeded to strut up and down across the green, his magnificent tail in full fan. I lost my heart entirely. Was this real, this bit of the opulent past?

After a while my aunt appeared, smiling still, but having the wisdom not to speak and break the spell. I climbed into the car, and we headed for home—and mint juleps made with old Maryland rye.

Today Wye House is owned by Mrs. Morgan Schiller, born Elizabeth Key Lloyd (Key from the family whose son gave us our national anthem). Mrs. Schiller grew up at Wye, and remembers spending quiet afternoons reading in the lovely graveyard, where so many generations of Lloyd children before her had come with tutors to do their lessons at the huge tables of stone.

As for my Orangery, it now serves as winter shelter for only two orange trees, both nurtured from pips by Mrs. Schiller heself. The ivy has grown up to cover the brick walls and push through the crevices of the window moldings; it now hangs inside in huge green draperies that sweep the floor. Furnished only with bales of sweet-smelling hay, the Orangery is still the home of Mr. and Mrs. Peacock and their child, whose ancestor I met long ago.

At Wye House: a scarlet garden cart, right, *by the graveyard gate; Suffolk sheep,* below, *grazing near the entrance drive*

The iridescent Mr. Peacock
strolling on the front lawn
of the Orangery, which
happens to be his home

The peaceful graveyard at
whose tablelike markers Wye
children did their studies
while young ladies embroidered
samplers and dreams

CHAPTER 2

The Wonders of Evergreen House, Baltimore, 1925-1935

IT WAS SPRING, and I had the traditional fever.

Somehow I found myself involved in a theatrical production for the Baltimore Junior League's annual charity dinner dance. I was to dance the tango with a lovely wisp of a girl named Mary Lawrason Riggs (there were to be dances of many nations, and since we were both slight and fair, we were naturally cast as the Argentines . . .). We were a huge success. So huge, in fact, that no sooner was I out of costume and back at my table in my black tie than I was collared by a friend and whisked to the table of the famous Ambassador and Mrs. John W. Garrett.

I had never met the Ambassador and his wife, Alice Warder Garrett, whom he had courted and married in Washington, but I had heard a great many fascinating stories about them and indeed about all that went on behind the tremendous gates of Evergreen, the family estate on Charles Street.

Alice Garrett eclipsed everyone at the table. She was olive-skinned, raven-haired, with flashing dark eyes and a generous red mouth, which, curiously, turned into a rectangle when she smiled. She was rather tall, slim-hipped but sturdily built, and conspicuously Paris dressed.

If I was worried about how to open the conversation, I needn't have been. Mrs. Garrett extended her hand to me as I approached.

"Ah," she said in her husky voice. "At last I have found you." I glanced nervously at Mr. Garrett, who gazed at me with unwavering steely blue eyes. Mrs. Garrett, it turned out, was looking for a partner for the dance recitals and musical programs she gave at her house. "Won't you come and dance with me?" she asked. The orchestra was striking up. "Why don't we dance right now?" she suggested. She was much bigger than I, and not exactly light as a feather, either. But she was so gay that the prospect was irresistible and I found myself agreeing to everything she said.

Two days later I was driving through those tremendous gates and onto the beautiful twenty-six-acre park that surrounds Evergreen. The car was well along into the rolling hilly grounds before I could even see the house, a pale-yellow brick classical revival building with soaring white columns grandly crowning the highest point of the property. The house had been built back in the 1850's but the Garrett family did not acquire it until 1878. They had begun adding on to it almost at once. I drove past the colonnade and under an archway to the entrance. The door was opened by a stiff butler in immaculate black livery that contrasted dramatically with the vestibule walls,

---

Note. The Evergreen House and collections are maintained by the Evergreen House Foundation and may be visited. Tours of the whole house are conducted periodically.

The original Evergreen House,
built in the 1850's

The annex, added as a
gymnasium and schoolroom,
later remodeled as a theatre.
Entrance is under the arch.

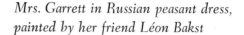

*Mrs. Garrett in Russian peasant dress,
painted by her friend Léon Bakst*

which were covered with Italian silk damask in a luscious cranberry red. There were many small pictures and drawings by contemporary artists, both European and American: Dufresne, George Grosz, Augustus John, Henry Varnum Poor, and Rivera. My Princeton days, which I had spent browsing through New York museums and galleries ("frittering away," my father called it), stood me in good stead now. There was also a portrait—of Mrs. Garrett's mother, I later learned—by Gari Melchers. The butler led me up five or six marble steps to a huge old tapestry hanging from a pole above our heads. It made an expensive rustling sound as he drew it back so we could pass through to the drawing room. I was charmed by this medieval remedy for drafts.

Once on the drawing-room side of the tapestry, I was instantly seized by a portrait, unmistakably of Mrs. Garrett, between the windows at the far end of the room. Zuloaga, the leading contemporary painter of Spain, had portrayed her in full Spanish regalia: white brocade skirt, white lace mantilla flowing from a white ivory comb. He had certainly captured the actress in her.

The drawing room, which was referred to quaintly as the parlor, was tall and narrow, with beige-colored walls, two fireplaces, and tall windows looking out on the tree-covered landscape. It was furnished with the typical stiff, pale, brocade-covered little sofas and chairs, a piano, and small rugs on a bare floor. It was pretty enough, but unremarkable except for the presence of the most amazing paintings. A Modigliani, a Bonnard, and, over the mantel, the first Picasso I had ever seen on anyone's wall. There was also an early Utrillo, and works by Derain, Segonzac, and Forain. And standing on an easel was another portrait—it must have been six feet tall—of Mrs. Garrett, looking beautiful in a blousy blue-and-white Russian peasant costume. It was painted by her friend Léon Bakst, and to this day I consider it one of the most elegant and lyrical portraits I have ever seen.

I was led through the parlor to a little chamber called the reading room, a strikingly ugly room with dark cherrywood paneling and convoluted, Tiffany-style plaster ceiling and cornice. At the far end, on a table, was yet another portrait of Mrs. Garrett—her face resting in cupped hands—by Jacques Émile Blanche. Beside the portrait sat Mrs. Garrett herself.

"Let's begin this relationship right," she said, before I could open my mouth. "If you are to be my dancing partner, we'll have none of this 'Mrs. Garrett' business. I am Alice; you are Billy."

"Very well, Alice," I said. Calling an older woman who was the wife of an ambassador by her first name tasted peculiar on my tongue.

She stood and smiled. "Come," she said. "I'll take you at once to the battlefield." Out the door and across the court we walked, to a building that was obviously newer than the house but attached to it by the archway I had driven under on my way in. The door of this annex opened to a long gallery, painted bright scarlet, lined with vitrines filled with Oriental porcelains and bronzes. This was known as the Far East Room, which, Alice said, had been built as a billiard room and bowling alley for the sons of some Garrett ancestor.

A small staircase led up to a kind of foyer, a fairly large room completely lined with mirrors, upon which hung no fewer than seventeen Dufy water colors. I was struck dumb—up to then I had seen Dufys only one at a time.

This room opened into a fantastically complete little theatre. Originally a gymnasium and small schoolroom, it had been converted by Léon Bakst in 1922 into a theatre for Mrs. Garrett's productions, with the schoolroom as a little stage.

It was a fabulous room. The walls were white with dark woodwork, and there were plenty of windows. Bakst had stenciled the white ceiling, supporting columns, and even the stage curtain in a joyous pattern of stylized birds and flowers in reds and oranges with black and green. It was delightfully rhythmic and even almost musical, an effect that Alice Garrett attributed to Bakst's years with the Ballet Russe. A great many costumes and stage settings for the little theatre were designed by Bakst himself, and others by the Mexican artist Miguel Covarrubias. For the audience there were rows of black-painted wicker chairs with shiny brown satin cushions.

I was astonished at the professionalism and completeness of everything. Even the intricate lighting system was first-rate, and operated by a skilled technician.

To one side of the stage was a corridor of small charming rooms painted white and furnished with bits of Federal furniture. This area had been affectionately dubbed the Geniuses' Wing because of the brilliant musicians who occupied it when they visited Evergreen.

Immediately beside the stage was a dressing room, complete with a theatrical make-up mirror and costumes by the ton. And on the opposite side was another room and bath with a full-length mirror.

"This will be your dressing room," said Alice Garrett. "We'll have to get you some nice costumes."

We walked back to the reading room, where Mr. Garrett joined us for tea. He was a calm, quiet man, whose gentleness, however, concealed a steel-trap intellect. I loved to listen to him speak in his distinct, clipped style, cultivated during his years in the diplomatic service. It was such a contrast to his wife's warm, throaty voice. I had not noticed before that he was rather bald and had a gray Vandyke beard. But

The theatre where Mrs. Garrett danced and sang. Bakst stenciled the walls, columns, even the ceiling, with his brilliant, whimsical designs.

The parlor, opposite, looking from the reading room. Above the door is one of Miguel Covarrubias's painted teak panels. In the library, right, a portrait of Mr. Garrett by Zuloaga hangs above the mantel.

no one could have missed the riveting blue eyes that put him in clear command of any situation. Just sitting there those few moments, quietly chatting with the Garretts, I came to realize that I had never known two people more completely in love; nor have I since. Each had a terrific respect for the other, and took an almost fierce pride in the other's accomplishments. If I had had any doubts about my dancing with the man's wife, they were erased at that tea table; Mr. Garrett welcomed me as enthusiastically as his wife had, because he knew I would give her pleasure. I suddenly felt very comfortable and happy.

That was the beginning of a ten-year friendship that included some of the most joyful moments of my life. The gates of Evergreen had opened up a whole new world to me. There I met many internationally celebrated people; there I was surrounded by the best art and music, as well as conversation. I knew I could never return to the life I had led before.

It was all settled; I was to come the very next afternoon to begin our serious work: the dancing. Miss Carol Lynn, Alice's teacher, taught us the steps to all the Spanish dances Alice loved, choreographed the numbers for our little performances, and commiserated with us when the going got tough. Our music was delightful Spanish piano recordings played on the Victrola.

Two portraits of Mrs. Garrett as a señorita, both by Zuloaga: *one in the hall,* above, *seen from the dining room; the other in the parlor,* right. *Above the chimneypiece hangs a Picasso; near the window, a Forain.*

It must be said that, although Alice Garrett had a delicious sense of humor, when we were engaged in our dancing rehearsals, all traces of it escaped her. She accepted without question the authority of her instructor, and studied her work in deadly earnest. Dancing with Alice Garrett was sometimes very strenuous. She was no mere wisp of a girl, and she had a definite will of her own. There were times when we did not exactly agree as to the music's rhythm. I hesitated at first to exert myself as a leader, in deference to the lady's age and position. After all, it was my good fortune to be dancing with her in the first place. But she soon put an end to that line of thinking.

"I want you to forget that my husband is a distinguished diplomat," she commanded. "When we are dancing, I am nothing but a Spanish girl, and I want you to treat me like one. I want you to throw me around a little."

I sized up the situation. The throwing around part was not going to be easy, but at least I could perhaps force her to step in time to the music. We began again. Miss Lynn demonstrated beautiful fluid movements and lots of graceful backbends. And, well, Alice tried.

We developed a tidy repertoire of dances. I danced only two with her; the rest were her solos. She had different costumes for each number. I myself had two: a beautiful matador suit of dark topaz-colored velvet with masses of thick gold braid, which I was to wear with horrendous but correct stockings in bull-ring pink, and long flared black velvet trousers and bolero worn over a ruffled white shirt.

Alice soon felt we were competent enough to perform before her public, and set a date. People were invited for a dinner to be followed by our performance in the Bakst Theatre. This might as well have been a Broadway debut, I was so nervous.

The dining room, which Bakst had decorated with brilliant Chinese yellow walls, tall dark doors and woodwork, and rather elaborate curtains of gold-and-magenta brocade, was dazzling the night of the party. On the walls was a set of eight seventeenth-century Chinese panels of magenta silk with a design in gilt. A group of priceless Chinese bronzes stood on the mantel; above them hung a Chinese painting on silk, dating from the Ming dynasty. This room, smaller in scale than others at Evergreen, could nevertheless seat twenty in great comfort. If more were coming, Alice would simply put up little tables all through the parlor.

That night the table was set with delicate gold-and-white Embassy crystal and gold plates. Unfortunately, the table far outclassed the food that was served on it; Alice Garrett had not the slightest interest in food. The people she invited all came anyway, of course, splendidly dressed and scintillating with jewels.

While everyone else was having dessert, Alice and I dashed for the dressing room, where Carol Lynn made me up like a Spaniard, complete with dark face powder and sideburns. The atmosphere was as hushed and electric as the wings of a New York stage. Presently, the guests took their places in the wicker chairs, and the curtain went

27

up. The sets were exciting, the lighting superb, the music delightful. The dancing, well, the dancing was performed with great enthusiasm and flair. Anyway, it didn't much matter; drinks were served during intermissions, and the Baltimoreans, sorry to say, were far more concerned with libation than with the arts.

Alice and I performed like this twice a season. If there were musicians staying at Evergreen at the time, they would play after the recital, or someone would sing, and everyone would have a lovely time.

Often Alice gave "classes" for the sole purpose of learning some new dance. We trooped up to the mirror-lined Dufy-decorated room to gape at ourselves dancing some new craze. We went through the Charleston in this way. Nothing is more threatening to one's self-image than to watch oneself doing the Charleston. Alice Garrett wasn't going to learn to dance from just anyone! She imported Ned Wayburn, the famous New York dancing teacher, to give us black-bottom lessons. We first saw the rhumba done by H. L. Mencken and the novelist Joseph Hergesheimer, two short round men who had learned the new step in Cuba that winter and danced it with the greatest possible solemnity while the rest of us crumpled up with laughter. If one happened to be a house guest at Evergreen when a new dance was being tried out, one was automatically included in the lessons. But there was also an intimate court that was always invited: Lucrezia Bori, the great Spanish soprano of the Metropolitan Opera, the architect Lee Taylor, probably the best dancer in Baltimore, and me.

Miss Bori, who was always referred to simply as Bori, was one of the wonders of Evergreen House—a small vivacious woman with the most beautiful manners. She had, unlike most sopranos of her day, an uncommonly pretty figure, which she dressed to great advantage. She had very sensitive hands and it was said that she wore white cotton gloves when she slept. Both Garretts loved her, and loved having her about.

When Alice decided she wanted to learn to sing, Bori consented to undertake the cultivation of her voice. This was no simple matter, since there wasn't much available raw material. But Alice was diligent and devoted, and eventually she was able to sing —if not like a nightingale, then at least with great style. She sang in Spanish and she sang in French, and the Spanish songs she sang were infused with the *brio* of Spain.

Now that singing was a part of Alice's repertoire, she naturally had to have special sets painted and costumes designed to go with each of her new numbers. One set was

The dining room, designed by Bakst

a replica of a Fragonard landscape, before which was hung a flower-trimmed swing ridden by Alice in shepherdess garb. Since I had nothing else to do during that particular number, I was recruited to stand behind the flats and pull on a rope that set Alice swinging back and forth over the audience.

During the years I visited Evergreen, the house itself underwent a few changes under the able direction of Alice. In 1928, three years after my first visit, a superb library was added on the far side of the reading room, creating a delightful enfilade of hall, parlor, reading room, and library unfolding perfectly, one into the other. The architect for this project was Laurence Hall Fowler, and the result was a standout. Everything was paneled in walnut, and there were six huge windows curtained in velvet that exactly matched the paneling. Over the marble mantel hung Zuloaga's portrait of Mr. Garrett in a relaxed pose, wearing a soft-blue smocklike shirt, which created a controversy among their friends, some of whom thought an ambassador should be painted in Napoleonic attire suitably adorned with medals. The parlor was henceforth to be used only for parties, and the library as the living room. The furniture was quiet: comfortable upholstered chairs and smallish sofas, and little chairs one could pull around to wherever they were needed—all in muted woody colors in leather or velvet, all very soft. The ample bookshelves held no fewer than eight thousand books (the entire house, I was told with pride, contained thirty-six thousand). Here and there on the bookshelves stood small masterpieces: a Rodin drawing, a Modigliani, and an early Picasso water color I coveted every time it caught my eye. Standing on another shelf was an old photograph of Mr. Garrett's grandfather, John W. Garrett, who had been president of the Baltimore & Ohio Railroad, with General McClellan and President Lincoln.

Four years after the library was added, Mr. Fowler came back to renovate the little reading room. Thank goodness! All that hideous cherry paneling was ripped off and replaced with natural teak. Large alcoves with huge sunny windows were built on, and furnished with leather reading chairs. On fan-shaped panels above the doors and leading to the alcoves were murals painted by Miguel Covarrubias—scenes of diplomatic posts held by Mr. Garrett in The Hague, Berlin, Paris, Rome, Argentina, Venezuela, Luxembourg, and Washington. They were painted right on the teak, and when the wood's lovely grain gleamed through in spots, the effect was charming.

The greatest gift the Garretts ever gave their friends was a series of concerts in the Bakst Theatre. Twice a year, in spring and fall, the Musical Arts Quartet performed for an hour every day for six weeks, alternating afternoons and evenings. I remember with total pleasure sitting in one of those comfortable chairs, feeling the warm breeze through the open windows, and listening to those lovely sounds. Over a period of years one could hear the entire library of string quartet music. Alice Garrett was always mistress of ceremonies for these concerts, and would introduce each number with the greatest dignity. And if she announced the wrong piece or got her composers mixed up, the first violinist would clear his throat, then solemnly correct her.

These concerts attracted some of the most brilliant figures in the world. Always in the audience among the Baltimore group were Mr. and Mrs. Jack Symington; Mr. and Mrs. Hamilton Owens, of the Baltimore *Sun*; Frank Kent and Mark Watson, the *Sun*'s great editorial writer; Lee Taylor and his wife, and Anne Kinsolving, who was courted at Evergreen by John Nicholas Brown of Providence, whom she later married. There were Drs. Baer, Welch, and Thayer, the great geniuses of Johns Hopkins Hospital, and Dr. Bowman, the President of Johns Hopkins University. Pauline Potter, who was to become the Baroness Philippe de Rothschild, was there, already the most glamorous and charming young woman in all of Baltimore. And the Garretts' best friends in Baltimore, Benjamin Howell Griswold, Jr., his son, Alexander Brown Griswold, and Gilman Paul.

From Washington came Mr. and Mrs. Robert Woods Bliss, who also had concerts by the Musical Arts Quartet at their house, Dumbarton Oaks, and Speaker of the House Nicholas Longworth and his wife, President Theodore Roosevelt's elder

One of the terraced gardens at Evergreen

daughter, Alice. George Garrett, a distant Washington cousin, was there, and Alice Garrett's sister, Mrs. Henry Leonard.

New York was represented at one time or another by Mr. and Mrs. Pierpont Moffatt, Mr. and Mrs. David K. E. Bruce, Mrs. Benjamin Rogers, and Mrs. Cole Porter.

People from all the arts flocked to the concerts. I met the painter Bernard Boutet de Monvel, the famous decorator Dorothy Draper, Walter Lippmann, Frank Crowninshield, Marc Connelly, and Frank Lloyd Wright. There was Tulio Carminati, the matinee idol of Italy, who became the heartthrob of the world when he played Grace Moore's leading man in *One Night of Love*; Walter Damrosch; the famous violinist Efrem Zimbalist with his wife, Alma Gluck; Leopold Stokowski with his pianist wife, Olga Samaroff, and Ernest Schelling, the well-known pianist and conductor. The most beautiful entrance I have ever seen was made into the theatre by the romantic Millicent Rogers, on the arm of her husband, Arturo Ramos.

The diplomatic corps at Evergreen concerts was no less impressive: among them, Arthur James Balfour, Robert Lansing, Joseph Grew, Anthony Eden, and, during the Garretts' sabbatical from Mussolini's Rome, Dino Grandi himself.

The first time I went to Evergreen during that sabbatical of theirs, I was greeted not by the dignified old black-suited butler, but by a dashing young footman in splendid green-and-gold livery, whom the Garretts had brought back with them from Rome. I noticed almost at once that Antonio had a special regard for his employer's wife, and he came to look upon me as something of an obstacle to his passions. Once, I arrived for tea at Alice's invitation and Antonio directed me to the garden, when in fact Alice was waiting in the library; the next time, he showed me to the library knowing full well she was in the garden. Both occasions delayed our meeting by forty-five minutes, which put Alice in a less than friendly mood. When we noticed Antonio's ill-disguised glee, we were able without difficulty to fit together the pieces of this rather Renaissance intrigue.

I managed to stay out of Antonio's way as much as possible. At one large cocktail party, however, it became necessary for us to work side by side for a few uncertain moments. Alice, owing to her own indifference to alcohol, said to me, "Be an angel, and help Antonio with the drinks. He's not very good at tending bar." Antonio led me rather grudgingly to the grog tray, where the *señora* had provided, for the drinking pleasure of her multitudinous guests, a total of two bottles of gin and a pitcher of orange juice. I was put in mind of a similar situation involving bread and a few fish. But since it didn't look as if any miracles were in the offing here, I descended with Antonio into the depths of the wine cellar in search of additional spirits. What a perfect place, I considered with a small shudder, for a murder, Italian style . . .

At one of our delayed tea parties, Alice told me all about the Roman wedding she had attended—the marriage of the Prince of Piedmonte, heir to the throne of Italy, to Princess Maria-José of Belgium. There was immense excitement and competition among the diplomats' ladies about the dresses for the grand occasion. As the wife of the American Ambassador, Alice felt a definite responsibility to turn herself out in fitting splendor. She took herself to Paris and put herself in the able hands of Mme Lanvin, who advised her that she could stand out even in that splendid crowd by wearing a dress, train, and veil all in the same spectacular color, but of various fabrics. Together they chose a celestial star-sapphire blue, with flecks of silver in the tiara and veil. I can't tell you how often I have put this advice to use in decorating. Variety can be created as much by texture as by so-called accent colors, which often serve only to distract from the over-all continuity.

I had recently launched my career as a decorator, and Alice encouraged me in many ways, asking my opinion and even my help in matters of curtains and cushions and other small things. Under no circumstances was I to entertain the idea of becoming a professional dancer. "You are a beautiful dancer," she said, "but promise me you will keep it, as I have, a special luxury." I knew exactly what she meant, and promised on the spot.

It is a rare thing when a woman like Alice Garrett can laugh at her own foibles. So many eccentric patronesses begin to take themselves so seriously that there is no room left for laughter. Alice could always laugh heartily at herself and in fact the greatest joke on Alice Garrett was one she took pleasure in telling against herself.

During one of her many trips to Paris, she met Marcel Proust, and quite characteristically wanted to get to know him better. She asked him to numerous dinners and teas, all of which Mr. Proust politely turned down with the excuse that his calendar was filled. Finally, in June, driven to desperation, she wrote him a note: "Will you give me the great pleasure of dining with me at the Ritz on the first Sunday in September?"

His reply came immediately: "Thank you so much for your kind invitation. Unfortunately I am unable to accept because that is the night I will be dining at the Ritz alone."

When I left for New York in 1935 to work with Ruby Wood, my Evergreen era came necessarily to an end. When, the following spring, I was invited to Evergreen, it was not as a performer or as a Baltimore host, but as a guest for a house party during the annual Maryland Hunt Cup; among the guests were Henry McIlhenny, of Philadelphia, and my old friend Lucrezia Bori. In enormous blue-and-white Chinese porcelain vases all through the library, reading room, and parlor were great branches of lilacs in every shade from palest lavender to deepest amethyst, and their heady fragrance filled the house, which it seemed to me, had never smelled or looked so beautiful.

33

CHAPTER 3

The Years with
Ruby Ross Wood,
1935-1950

IT WAS APRIL 1930, and the night of the Maryland Hunt Cup Ball. A spring rain was falling, and the ballroom, although filled with laughter and music, was quite chilly. Mrs. Thomas Symington, whose house I had just decorated, came up to me and asked if I would please come to her table to meet one of her house guests, a woman by the name of Ruby Ross Wood. My heart leapt. There was no name that meant more to me, no human being I wanted more to meet. As a boy I had clipped everything she wrote for *Vogue* and *House & Garden*, and I knew she had also once been a reporter for a Georgia newspaper and a sometime ghost writer. Mrs. Wood had learned decorating entirely on her own, and had gone on to become the *doyenne* of the first great department-store decorating department: *Au Quatrième*, on the fourth floor of Wanamaker's. I couldn't believe I was actually going to meet her now.

My theart thumping wildly, I followed Mrs. Symington through the thicket of glittering dancers to her table on the far side of the floor. The ballroom was a brilliant scene of bejeweled ladies in the prettiest thirties' dresses, quite décolleté, and their men, mostly in pink tail coats—all dancing among white damask-covered tables with bowls of scarlet tulips on them. It was amid all this splendor that I first saw my goddess; she was sitting at the table, wrapped in a rumpled raincoat.

Mrs. Wood looked up at me very shyly. She was round and soft-looking, with a little gray fluff of hair and eyes that snapped behind the biggest pair of horn-rimmed spectacles imaginable, with lenses tinted faintly pink! She told me later that when she was in London on a buying trip for Wanamaker's, Rosa Lewis, owner of the famous Cavendish Hotel, referred to her as " 'er with the glasses." I was to discover that with those eyes " 'er with the glasses" was capable of reducing to ashes anyone who crossed 'er.

Mrs. Wood extended to me one of the most beautiful hands I think I have ever seen: slender, sensitive, with perfect nails, and wearing on one finger a gigantic cabochon ruby.

"If we ever recover from this damned Depression," she said in a soft sweet voice, "I would like you to come to New York and work with me." I was stunned: work with Ruby Ross Wood? "I'm staying with Edith Symington," she went on, "and Edith tells me everything in the house is entirely your fault." (This was not completely true: the furniture the Symingtons owned came from everywhere in the world, and provided me with one of my rare chances in Baltimore to work with other than strictly English furniture.) "The house has made me realize that I need a man as my associate."

I sailed through the rest of the evening on a little cloud. After that, whenever I went to New York I always stopped by at Mrs. Wood's office just to say hello—and to keep myself in her mind. Five years later, she telephoned me at the Baltimore decorating firm where I worked.

"Mr. Baldwin, this is Ruby Wood," she said in her sweet voice. "I would like you to have lunch with me tomorrow."

I said, delighted, "Where?"

"At the top of the Pierre."

"In New York?"

"In New York."

I went, of course, expecting great things. A strange lunch: I behaved like a positive jumping jack, doing my best to charm the woman, but thinking the whole time, When on earth are we going to talk about that job? Mrs. Wood watched and listened, not uttering a single word until the very end. "Will you come with me to see my shop?" she said.

Off we went to Madison Avenue and Fifty-seventh Street. I followed her into her private office, where she walked directly to her desk, put down her bag, and took out a cigarette.

"I want you to come and work for me," she said with her back toward me, "but I cannot pay you anything."

"What do you mean?" I asked. She handed me a sheet of pink paper.

"Here is your contract," she said.

"Your salary will be thirty-five dollars a week," the extraordinary document read. "You will have the use of my husband's and my apartment until the first of November, because we will be living in Long Island until then. You will have a maid who will take care of you, do your laundry, make your breakfast, and every afternoon when you come home from work, there will be a grog tray set up for Martinis."

I said, "I have to ask my mother."

A month later, on July 8, 1935, I left home, bound for New York. My dear mother had added to Mrs. Wood's thirty-five dollars a week another fifteen. (I suspected it was worth *at least* that much to her to get me out of the house.)

I went right to the apartment of Ruby Wood and her husband, Chalmers, at 277 Park Avenue. The building covered an entire city block and was quite notorious in those days. Unofficially, it was known as the Acre of Love because a great many rather stylish gentlemen kept little establishments there for ladies of whom they were fond. The door to the Woods' flat was opened by a short, fat Indian woman with a peaceful face. She was Minnie, a princess of the Matinecoc tribe of Long Island Indians. She showed me to my room, asked what I would like for breakfast, and informed me that I would never again see her. In the mornings there was always a little tray for me in the pantry with a toaster, some bread, honey, and coffee ready to be put on the fire. In the evenings when I came home, everything was immaculate,

36

Love to dear Billy from Ruby Ross Wood —
1939

Mrs. Wood, above, fully
engrossed at her solitaire
table in Long Island, and
at her desk in her New
York office, dressed in her
usual costume: veiled hat,
clanking gold bracelet,
round rose-colored glasses

A gathering of tastemakers at a party at Amster Yard, May 22, 1946. Above, *from left:* Mrs. Edna Woolman Chase, editor of VOGUE; Mrs. Benjamin Rogers; Woodson Taulbee; Albert Kornfeld, editor of HOUSE & GARDEN; Mrs. Wood, and me pouring champagne. Right, *from left:* James Amster, Miss Marian Hall, Mrs. Wood, Mrs. Wood's young associate Billy Baldwin, William Pahlmann, Mrs. Dorothy Draper, and Miss Nancy McClelland

and the only evidence that Minnie had been there was the little grog tray laid out for me with fresh glasses, gin, and vermouth. There was a flask of absinthe on the tray, too, because, as I was soon to learn, Chalmers Wood thought a tiny dash of this poisonous liquid gave Martinis an incomparable flavor. The beautiful globular tumblers were made of Irish silver, not glass, because Mrs. Wood felt silver kept Martinis colder. I did in fact see Minnie again, once, in the middle of a terrific midnight thunderstorm; awakened by the thunder, I saw a dark round shadow quietly and quickly closing my window.

The apartment where I spent that first summer was extraordinarily comfortable. Comfort was the primary principle of all Mrs. Wood's decorating; her motto was "Decorating is the art of arranging beautiful things comfortably." To a client who had come to her with two possible ways of decorating a house, she replied without the slightest hesitation: "We will consider only the one that is most comfortable." This insistence on comfort was bred into Mrs. Wood from her childhood in Georgia; she was very much at one with the Old South, and felt people should always feel at home, at ease. She thought that hospitality should be almost tangible.

The Woods' white living room was filled with upholstered furniture, all covered in blue-and-white-striped bed ticking—the first time this underestimated fabric had ever been used in decorating. The curtains were also made of ticking, and the floor was lacquered white, with several brown-and-white Moroccan rugs. At one end of the room was a white-painted table twelve feet long with a scalloped apron, and on it were piles and piles of magazines—*House & Garden, Vogue, Harper's Bazaar*; the Woods were great friends of Carmel Snow, Condé Nast, and Edna Woolman Chase. It was on this table that I found my grog tray every evening, set by the invisible Minnie. Here and there on tables around the room were large lamps of very inexpensive dark-blue porcelain with white paper shades. There were many personal photographs grouped on tables, and a few drawings on the walls. And, in the chilly days of October, always fresh bundles of wood by the fireplace, which Mrs. Wood had forgotten to mention in my contract.

During my years with Ruby Ross Wood, she and Chalmers lived in three different apartments at 277 Park. They found, of course, a very good excuse for each move they made: lack of light, lack of space, and so on. But one did not have to be very bright to figure out the real reason: Mrs. Wood wanted to decorate. Those apartments were really little laboratories for her.

In the last one they had, Mrs. Wood created a room that became famous. It was entirely red. The floors were carpeted wall to wall in a dark damson color, the walls *strié* the color of a rich red currant. There were ruby-red satin curtains and a great deal of tufted Victorian furniture exactly the color of a Harvard-red carnation. The small things—pillows, lamps, boxes, objects—ran the whole spectrum of red, with bright punctuations of scarlet. All the pictures were contemporary, many of them painted by the Woods' friends. The room was pleasantest in winter, with snow falling and the view of the Grand Central Tower—sadly to be obliterated by the Pan American Building—very baroque indeed.

The bed I slept in, which was Chalmers's, was covered in scarlet serge, and next to it was an enormous bedside table not with a table lamp on it, but a floor lamp standing beside it. I confess that the idea of standing lamps was anathema to me, and more than that, a symbol of bad taste. But Ruby Wood had created the simplest straight shafts of black iron with absolutely plain paper shades that gave both direct and indirect light, the kind of light she thought best for in-bed reading. And, although the lamps did not entirely change my feelings about standing lamps, they were really perfectly fine. There was also a small low black leather Knole sofa, which I liked to sit on while putting on my shoes and which, no doubt, Chalmers liked to sit on for putting on *his* shoes. That first evening I used it to take *off* my shoes. I then unpacked my suitcases, padded out in slippers to have a bite of supper, which Minnie had left for me, and fell blissfully into bed. Life in the big city had begun.

I arrived at work next morning in time to welcome Mrs. Wood, who had just got in from the country. Her chauffeur, Paul, carried in buckets and buckets of flowers from the gardens and greenhouses. The flowers were mostly irises, and ranged in color from the palest blue to the deepest purple-black. Mrs. Wood loved flowers to the point of madness, and the office was always full of them. The irises never looked better than in Mrs. Wood's office, which was painted a very pale icy blue, with the furniture slip-covered in navy cotton moire. Mrs. Wood had arranged the objects for sale on tables entirely by color, not by texture or purpose or period. They were like great bouquets of chairs and fabrics and objects, one bouquet of all the shades of red, another of yellow, another of lilac, and so on all through the spectrum.

I was surprised to see that Mrs. Wood was wearing a rather heavy black wool coat. It was mid-July and very warm. When she took the coat off, she put on a sweater. And it wasn't, I learned, that she was simply cold that day; she was *always* cold. Mrs. Wood carried this little quirk of hers to astounding lengths: when she motored back and forth from Long Island, even during the summer months, she wore a sweater, a coat, and a fur, and sealed all the car windows. Her fellow passengers not only baked in the heat but were asphyxiated as well, for Mrs. Wood was never without a cigarette. I never knew anyone to smoke so much. The fluff of bangs that touched the top of her glasses was actually tinged at the edges with a pale smoky red from the nicotine of that steady stream of tobacco.

That day, Mrs. Wood was wearing what would become a familiar costume to me: a simple black wool dress with a beautiful red silk scarf tied at her throat and fastened with a huge cabochon ruby like the one in her ring. Sometimes the scarf varied in hue,

Architect William Adams Delano,
painted by Bernard Boutet de Monvel,
with Little Ipswich as the background

but it never went out of the blue-red range. Although she dressed simply, she had given her wardrobe some thought. "I do not dress like a cook," she told me once. "I dress like a clubwoman." I rarely saw Mrs. Wood without a hat. They were usually small, sometimes made entirely of tiny flowers, and often had veils.

Her jewelry was simple: every morning she arrived at the office wearing an enormous jangly gold bracelet on which hung heavy gold eighteenth-century wax seals—and the first thing she did was walk to her desk and remove it.

Her beautiful hands were always a source of fascination. She carried a gold cigarette case in a little black suède slip cover. I will never forget her hands, moving gracefully, regally, opening that case to remove or refill its deadly contents. She relied as heavily on her sense of touch as most people do on their sight. She touched everything; if it was beautiful to the touch, then she knew it must be truly beautiful.

My first assignment at Ruby Ross Wood, Inc., was to spend a month going to antique dealers and wholesale houses selecting things I liked and making notes of them. After the month was over, Mrs. Wood and I went to the dealers together. At each place she would settle herself in a chair and say, "Now show me." It was her way of discovering what my taste and preferences were.

It wasn't long before I was allowed to decorate my own office. I can't tell you how excited I was about that! I painted the wall dark brown (the color that has haunted me all my life). I had a little Sheraton sofa covered in dappled leather, like the old gray mare, and a remarkable pair of Italian busts of Carlotta and Maximilian wearing the most peculiar expressions. On the wall above the sofa hung Louis Reynal's very first

41

photomural: a blowup of a faïence horse against a background of cloudy sky.

In the beginning I worked closely with Mrs. Wood on her own jobs, taking notes, doing her installations, learning everything about decorating in New York, which was in many ways the same as, but in many ways quite different from, decorating in Baltimore. Although Mrs. Wood was the head of her business, she refused to learn anything about the actual business side. She shivered at the very sound of the word bill, and refused to talk about one or even to present one. She never did her own estimates; nor, as a matter of fact, did she ever install any of the rooms she designed. Mrs. Wood "created" and went home. It was up to the rest of us—and I must say she had a devoted staff—to work up the estimates, set up the rooms, and bill the clients. As a result, I learned every aspect of the business of interior decoration.

Toward the end of my grace period in the Woods' apartment on Park Avenue, Mrs. Wood was working day and night with Mr. and Mrs. Wolcott Blair to finish their Palm Beach house. She had agreed to do a house for another client there as well, but found that she did not have the time.

"Billy, I am simply too busy" she said. "I want you to do the house."

I felt at that moment something close to joy, but just as close to terror. I showed her everything I was planning to do, and, to my great delight, she was well pleased.

Thus, after four months of working with Mrs. Wood, I was on my own in more ways than one: since the Woods were about to move back to town for the winter, I went and found myself a little railroad apartment on Sutton Place, in a lovely row of black-and-white houses with brightly painted doors—a ravishing little complex that was later torn down to make room for one of New York's famous ghastly apartment buildings. In addition to these manifestations of my coming of age, my salary was suddenly jumped, much to my mother's relief, to the dazzling sum of one hundred and twenty-five dollars a week. For me, at least, the damned Depression was over.

Through the years with Ruby Wood, I learned that she was one of the most impatient, intolerant people. Although her voice was soft, and her Southern origin charmingly betrayed itself in certain delightfully drawled words, they just barely concealed an intolerance that was almost legendary. She was extremely shy herself, but she abhorred timidity in others. And thoughtlessness was at the top of her sin list. One Christmas morning when I called to say Merry Christmas, she complained: "Billy, so far the presents my friends have given me are all duds. It's not the gift that counts, it's the lack of thought behind it."

One day a woman we had never seen before appeared at the office with the plans of her new apartment. I sat dutifully by with pad and pencil. The woman began: "I want the apartment to look exactly like the one Dorothy Draper did for a friend of mine."

Mrs. Wood stood up and regarded the woman with a look so sharp it threatened to shatter those famous glasses. "Mrs. Draper's office is two blocks away," she said icily. "Mr. Baldwin will give you the exact address." The woman folded her plans and made for the door in a panic.

Even when she was just beginning her career, Ruby Ross Wood could not control herself. There was once an absurd fashion of having curtains hang down the wall and then flow onto the floor ("breaking" on the floor, in decorator talk); I can even remember with horror seeing somewhere pink taffeta curtains held in place by a taffeta-upholstered brick! Mrs. Wood had as a client a well-known, difficult *nouvelle riche* who insisted on having such curtains for her country house. Since it was Mrs. Wood's first really big job, she was forced to comply. When the job was done, the woman had one complaint: "The curtains are not long enough."

"It seems to me," said Mrs. Wood, "that they are very much on the floor."

"Don't you realize," said the woman, "that people's incomes are judged by the amount of curtain they have on the floor?"

"Well," said Mrs. Wood—and I can just see the look in those eyes of hers—"in that case, my dear, yours have got to go all across the room, through the foyer, out the door, and," she continued, picking up her bag to leave, "good-by!"

Later, in self-defense, she developed a sense of humor about her clients, and was able to laugh at the idiocy of the woman who, two days after the French bed she had insisted on was delivered, came in to complain: "The Louis XV bed is too small. I think I'd better get a Louis XVI."

For all her pronounced intolerance, I have never known anyone to be as generous as Ruby Ross Wood about the work of other decorators. Whenever she received an announcement that a new shop was to open, she went absolutely wild and could not sit still until she saw it. If she approved the work, her encouragement and enthusiasm were boundless; if she disapproved, she was, of course, just as vocal in her scorn. She would write encouraging notes—she was a great note writer—to the young decorators on charming pink note paper engraved in scarlet. When Niki de Gunzburg, then editor of *Town and Country*, published a large picture of a child's birthday-party table, Mrs. Wood wrote to him that the picture was "a child's dream forever." And Niki has kept that note all these years. And when I was away in the army, I got those little pink notes twice a week.

If Mrs. Wood could not take on a job, she would never hesitate to recommend someone else. She was the first decorator asked to design the sets for *Gone With the Wind*. She became as excited as a child at the prospect, but her impossible schedule forced her to decline; she recommended Joseph B. Platt, whom she greatly admired, and Mr. Platt got the job. Mrs. Wood never had the slightest jealousy of me once I was on my own. She always gave credit exactly where and when it was due.

She could afford to—she was quite simply the finest decorator who ever lived. Her ideas were always *avant-garde*; her capacity for innovation astounding. At a time

43

Mrs. Wood's bedroom at Little Ipswich. Above her bed, framed lantern slides that once belonged to Marie Antoinette; beside it, that fringed lamp shade

when white was not used, she used lots of white. When pastel and muted shades were the vogue, she brilliantly colored rooms as backgrounds for antiques. She never overdecorated. She felt that if the decoration imposed itself on your eye or made itself the topic of conversation it was no good. She avoided trends and styles at all costs and taught me to do the same.

"Never adopt a particular style and peddle it as your own," she told me. "Always be personal, always be flexible. Many decorators fall into a trap, and when they finally want to do something a little different, they find they cannot because their clients have stereotyped them."

Mrs. Wood never stopped discovering new things. In the fall of 1936, she returned from abroad clutching five or six lengths of cloth—cotton, printed in the freshest, most brilliant flower colors I had ever laid eyes on—all designed by Mme Paule Marrot of Paris. This was a dazzling break from the muted antique tones everyone was using, and Mrs. Wood put the materials into operation directly.

She called the talented Margaret Owen, a colleague of hers from the old Wanamaker days and a fellow rose lover (roses were, of course, Mrs. Wood's favorite flower). At that time Miss Owen was an importer of papers and materials from France, and Mrs. Wood suggested to her that she become the New York representative of Paule Marrot. Miss Owen jumped at the idea, and that is how these ravishing printed bouquets on fabric and wallpaper (many of them matching—another

innovation) came across the Atlantic, changing my color palette forever.

One time Mrs. Wood and I decided to start a line of materials of our own. Mrs. Wood's brother-in-law, Harry Cimino, was quite a brilliant artist with woodcuts. Together he and Mrs. Wood designed wonderful cotton chintzes, which he then hand-screened. We sold them with great success to all the other decorators.

Mrs. Wood couldn't help being innovative. One Christmas, when she was working at Wanamaker's and everyone was giving each other presents wrapped in red or green paper with maybe a little fake holly, Mrs. Wood put on Rodman Wanamaker's desk a little present wrapped in silver paper and tied with silver ribbon and a little cluster of silver Christmas balls. Toward noon of that very day, a memo went around summoning everyone in the decorating department to Mr. Wanamaker's office that afternoon.

"I want to show you all something I consider a real event, a thing of great imagination, which I think is going to revolutionize the whole standard of Christmas wrapping," he told the group. He held up Mrs. Wood's present. "We can see from this small box that wrapping can be made personal and have as much fantasy and magic as the present itself." The present was passed around, oohed and ahed over, and then returned to Mr. Wanamaker's desk, where it sat unopened for several months. He considered the wrapping alone a great gift. To her dying day, Mrs. Wood never knew whether Mr. Wanamaker ever found out what was inside!

Mrs. Wood was an exhibitor in the Decorators' Picture Gallery, one of the annual New York winter events of the thirties. The Decorators' Picture Gallery was a space rented by the Davison sisters, Mrs. Ward Cheney and Mrs. Artemus Gates.

Decorators would choose pictures at certain galleries and then design rooms for them using any schemes they pleased. The exhibition would be open to the public during two months in winter. Mrs. Wood once did a sensational sitting room in pink-and-white stripes, the glory of which was a white plaster mantel molded to look as if it were swathed in white cloth and standing against a totally mirrored overmantel. The room was a knockout. The ladies were ecstatic.

At the end of my very first week with Mrs. Wood, she took me to her house at Syosset, Long Island, for the weekend. Inspired by the gatehouse of Kimolton Castle in England, the house—called Little Ipswich because Chalmers came from Ispwich, Massachusetts—had been adapted by William Adams Delano. It was a small white pavilion in the center of three wonderful vistas of the countryside that Long Island then boasted. The approach was through thick woodlands, and then suddenly the car turned sharply into a driveway lined with linden trees, clipped into great green cubes, all the way to the entrance court. Across the court rose the dome of the entrance hall, surmounted by a weathervane in the form of a golden swan. Mr. Delano was so proud of the house that when he asked Bernard Boutet de Monvel to paint his portrait, he chose it as the background.

I could see at once that the house was a rare beauty. Under the dome of the circular entrance hall stood full-scale terra-cotta figures of the four seasons alternating with tall windows curtained in Italian silk of palest blue, patterned with white stars. Golden swans were painted around the rim of the dome. And opposite the front door was another, which gave onto a terrace and the pond, home for a family of swans.

To the left of the hall was the dining room, tall and white, with a concave wall into which was set a beautiful white marble Adam chimneypiece. The curtains were of deep-blue damask patterned with large white swans; there were swan motifs on the silver candelabra and compotes—there were, in fact, swans all over the house! One of the guest rooms, which was painted a pale shrimp pink, had a bed with posts crowned by swan finials painted silver and then glazed to become silver gilt. As we were having lunch in the dining room one day, with the garden door open, into the room swept a hugh male swan, hissing and flapping in the most terrifying manner. Having once seen a swan break a woman's arm with its wing, I had no wish to be in the presence of an ill-humored swan ever again. Chalmers convinced it that Leda was not among the guests, and showed it to the door.

Around the oval Irish Chippendale table were eight high-back leather armchairs; Mrs. Wood felt it was insulting for the host and hostess and not the guests to have armchairs, and therefore established equal comfort for all.

The food served at that table was among the best I have ever eaten. It was simple, and a lot of it dated from Mrs. Wood's upbringing in the South: corn bread, spoon bread, and other luscious conceits, some of which I remembered with joy from my

The living room at Little Ipswich. Panel on left-hand wall was
one of three in the room, all painted on leather by John Wootton.

own youth. Chalmers's favorite was Clams Southside, brought from the Southside Club in nearby Islip, where he had once lived. There was, however, one glaring omission from the menu: soup.

"I hope you are not insane about soup," Mrs. Wood told me one day when we were alone, "because you will never have any in this house. On our honeymoon Chalmers ate soup, and I cannot tell you the noise he made. Rather than speak to him about it, I determined never to have soup in this house." And she never did.

To the right of the hall, a long corridor hung with glorious eighteenth-century Chinese wallpaper led to the living room. This was a large white room decorated with painted leather panels of sporting scenes done by John Wootton. The furniture and curtains were all in various shades of almondy green, and the French Savonnerie carpet was all in muted yellow-greens, brilliantly accented with orangey coral. I was struck at once by the position of the piano, which Mrs. Wood had placed perpendicular to the wall rather than conventionally parallel. A large comfortable armchair backed up to the piano and, in place of the piano bench, Mrs. Wood had a little bastard chair covered with needlepoint. Noel Coward spent the weekend with Mrs. Wood some years later and called the chair "Queen Victoria as a little girl."

Mrs. Wood always used lots of silver for sparkle: wine coolers, bowls, candlesticks. She loved to arrange flowering branches in the wine coolers; there would be short-clipped apple-blossom boughs in spring, and then, soon afterward, lovely branches of pink laurel. In one enormous bay window were masses of magnificent pink and red geranium plants, which never seemed to stop blooming the whole year round.

Shortly after my first visit, Mrs. Wood slip-covered all the green furniture in cream-colored chintz with beige-and-white roses and almond-green leaves. It was then that the drawing room was at its most beautiful.

Mrs. Wood's own bedroom had an inlaid Italian Directoire floor in a pattern of circles and stars. The walls were pale green, and there was a wonderful Sheraton bed painted black and hung with oyster-white silk. On the wall above the bed hung two framed fragments of a lantern slide that once belonged to Marie Antoinette. That room could be reproduced today and seem totally undated except for one thing: the lamp shade, which was a very elaborate silk affair with fringe. I am positive Mrs. Wood would never have it today. (This only goes to support my oft-repeated axiom that nothing in decoration is more the victim of fashion than lamp shades.)

Whenever Mrs. Wood was in the Long Island house, she would install herself at a particular card table with a sensible standing lamp. Here she would sit, never budging except to eat and sleep. Doing what? Playing solitaire. Solitaire was her relaxation and all her exercise. (I never saw her take any real exercise except for a walk in the woods once a year to inspect the candelabra primroses she had planted there.)

Years later, when she was too ill even to play cards, Mrs. Wood spent hours in front of that amazing new invention, the television; she was utterly fascinated with this innovative new medium that could snatch pictures right out of the air. She became, curiously, an avid baseball fan. She died in the winter of 1950; just a year later her devoted Chalmers died, literally of a broken heart. They had spent their first night in their beloved house on January 28, 1929, and had been there happily together for twenty-one years. On the first page of the guest book, Mrs. Wood had written:

God bless this little house of ours
And keep it filled with friends and flowers
And song and music, talk and books,
And not too many changing cooks.
We pray our ponds may ever flow,
Our two swans live for evermore,
Our woods give us sweet-smelling logs
Our days be gay with friendly dogs.
Our horses always to our mood,
Our larder never fail us food.
Our birds sing on, and never cease,
Our woods and paths for paths of peace.
God rest us merry, keep us well,
And give us many days to dwell
Within these walls. God give us wit
To make the very best of it.

On the second page of the guest book, William Delano, their adored and revered architect, wrote a poem that not only summed up the beautiful relationship they had, but also epitomized the sentiments of all of us who knew and loved Mrs. Wood:

Together we have planned this house
With love have sought, in brick and stone
To model here a perfect home
So fashioned that the shadows fall
In pleasant patterns on the wall,
And so disposed that rooms have sun,
With space and air in every one.
It's finished . . . Only time can tell
Whether we've done it ill or well.
For me, who love both you and it
The time has come to write "exit."
Before I leave one thing I do:
Pray God that peace may be with you.

CHAPTER 4

Inside a Lacquer Box: Mrs. Walter Farwell's Sitting Room, 1935

THE FIRST WEEKEND I ever spent with Ruby Ross Wood at her house on Long Island, she simply couldn't sit still until I promised to let her show me a favorite room of hers, which happened to be in the house of her friend, Mrs. Walter Farwell. Mrs. Farwell had furnished and decorated the room—the whole house—entirely by herself, and this seemed to make Mrs. Wood doubly proud and eager to show it off.

The house was a long graceful Georgian beauty built of lovely pale-pink brick. We walked up a gradual flight of stone steps to a broad terrace, thickly planted with beds of heliotrope, that ran the whole length of the house. If I shut my eyes, I can still see the delicate lavender against the faded brick, still breathe that warm fragrance.

The front door opened into a traditionally huge Georgian entrance hall. To one side was the drawing room, pure Adam, and to the other, a lovely dining room done in pale greens and made startlingly personal by curtains of unlined navy-blue linen to temper the summer sun.

The jewel of the house, however, was just a small sitting room.

A lacquer box, as all lovers of beautiful things know, is a small treasure designed to hold smaller treasures. Imagine my delight when I found myself standing inside one.

I never realized there could be such a variety of shine. The gleaming paneled walls were lacquered a perfect Coromandel black-brown (a color I fell in love with at once and have never gotten over; my own apartment today is painted that same deep shiny brown). Two lovely old Chinese lacquer flower paintings were set into the overmantel panel, their original gloss aged to a deep glow; a screen made of four paintings very like one another was set into the space above the sofa. Two lofty windows across the room sparkled, curtainless, in the sun.

Softly gleaming beige satin covered all the upholstered furniture except one little gem of a miniature wing chair, which was covered in delicious peach-colored antique Chinese brocade. One of the satin chairs was a small Elsie de Wolfe slipper chair, originally designed for a bedroom, but not in the least ashamed to appear in public.

On the fireplace wall stood a pair of black lacquer corner cabinets. Across the room (visible in the mirror) stood a screen upholstered in another old, peachy brocade. The shiny floor was covered with the only things in the room that didn't shine: a pale, intricate Oriental rug, very old, in a bouquet of beiges and apricots, and, near the sofa, a tiny rug that wasn't a rug at all, but an old Chinese saddle blanket.

"Well, what did you think?" Mrs. Wood asked, her eyes sharp behind her rosy lenses, as we walked down the heliotrope-scented path.

"I think," I said, "that if that room were reproduced fifty years from now, it wouldn't be a bit dated." She smiled, not needing to ask me why.

Mrs. Walter Farwell's lacquer box

CHAPTER 5

Pleasure Dome in Palm Beach: The Wolcott Blair House, 1936

ON A HANDSOME PATCH of Palm Beach—that manicured island between placid Lake Worth and the sea—Mr. and Mrs. Wolcott Blair decided to build their winter house.

They were the Blairs of Chicago, where they lived in a beautiful house designed by their good friend David Adler, who, when he learned of the property in Palm Beach, made them a present of plans for a house he had intended to build for his wife —plans he abandoned when she died tragically. Mr. and Mrs. Blair accepted this great gift from their friend, for they knew it would be the perfect house. To ensure its perfection, they asked Ruby Ross Wood to help them decorate it.

One approached the H-shaped house through a generous courtyard and entered it through one of the wings. Straight ahead, up a flight of stairs, was the long sunlit drawing room that formed the crossbar of the H. It was like being on a kind of furnished glass bridge that looked westward across the patio, pool, and lawn to Lake Worth, eastward to the lawn and beach (reached via tunnel under South Ocean Boulevard) and the sea.

The elevation of the living room permitted an entire mechanical complex to be built beneath it, level with the pool terrace: here were changing rooms and baths for the pool, and, most remarkable of all, an ingenious water-pump system that enabled the enormous arched drawing-room windows to be lowered completely to the ground.

Even before the decoration, the house was superb with its brilliant architecture. It needed very little embellishment—and that's just what it got.

The color of the drawing room was buff, pale, almost not there at all. The trim was purest white, and the floors ancient Cuban marble the color of parchment. The flooring was a near disaster: not enough marble squares arrived from Cuba to cover the whole area and there was no more. Mrs. Wood solved the problem by making a border all around of pale bleached oak. If she had planned it from the beginning, it couldn't have been more successful.

The decoration was pared down to the essentials of beauty and comfort—an appropriate scheme for a house in the tropics, but also proof that simplicity does not age: any of the rooms could be published in a current magazine and never betray that they were designed and lived in in 1936. Mrs. Wood and the Blairs had an uncanny sense of classicism, and together they conspired to strike at the heart of timelessness.

The drawing room was furnished comfortably but sparsely. In the very center of the cool bare floor stood a great writing table, its beauty achieved at the small cost of a simple pale fruitwood Louis XV frame and, for the top, a scalloped slip cover made of honey-brown leather edged with common white carpet tape. Grouped around were chairs covered to match. Several upholstered chairs were slip-covered in Elsie de Wolfe's famous leopard chintz; sofa covers and curtains were made of a simple heavy-textured beige cotton from Sweden. A pair of Adam cabinets of palest stripped pine stood at one end of the room, and scattered throughout were small tables and a few old wood-framed chairs, all of English origin, all upholstered in quiet no-colors. To light the room, there were the simplest possible white porcelain lamps, plus four carved wood *torchères* in the shape of palm trees.

At intervals down the length of the room, tall white lilies (from Cuba, since there was a general laziness in Florida about flower growing) nodded in wonderful big tubs. These washtubs were imported in their natural galvanized state from a hardware store in West Palm Beach, then coated and recoated with white lacquer. To the left of the staircase in the entrance wing was the library, a personal sitting room facing the sea where the Blairs could be alone or with a few intimate friends. The library was beautifully proportioned, cool, and tall. The walls were painted and glazed the color of bone—very white, but very soft; the carpetless floor was contemporary parquet in a beautiful rich chestnut. For the curtains and most of the furniture, Mrs. Wood used an English chintz of rather strong bright-blue flowers on a white background. By the window stood an extraordinary scarlet lacquer desk, an eighteenth-century *meuble*; Mrs. Blair had bought it years before from Elsie de Wolfe herself.

One white-carpeted guest room was painted a barely discernible blue. Only one fabric was used in the room: a delightful pale-blue chintz with fluffy white carnations and dark-green leaves. Mrs. Wood thought it would be fun to paint the chest of drawers to match.

In the far wing, across the drawing-room bridge, was Mrs. Blair's own bedroom, which also looked out to sea. The walls were tinted so slightly pink that they appeared white. The bedcover was beige linen, completely filled with exquisite trapunto embroidery. Most of the furniture was done in creams, off-white, or beiges; the curtains were of ice-cream-pink cotton satin from Syrie Maugham's London shop. There was a small collection of very good eighteenth-century drawings, an Aubusson rug of pinks and beiges and lovely soft brown, and, on the writing desk, two lamps made of crystal blocks—very much of the thirties *and* the seventies.

The house was as chic as it was comfortable, and would be in as perfect taste today as it was the day the Blairs moved in.

The guest room: white carnations printed on pale-blue fabric,
with a chest of drawers painted to match

The drawing room, all done in textures of beige and white.
Opposite: Mrs. Blair's pale-pink bedroom

The pleasure dome as it looked from the ocean, above, and from Lake Worth.
Opposite: *the white library with its blue-and-white chintz, immaculate bare floor*

CHAPTER 6

Fantasy in Jamaica, September 1938

IN SEPTEMBER OF 1938, I set out for a part of the world I had never seen before: the Caribbean Sea and the island of Jamaica. The day I left New York there was another historic departure—Sir Neville Chamberlain flew from London to Munich for his famous talks with Hitler.

The train pulled into Miami on Sunday afternoon. The air was hot and forebodingly still—not even a whisper of a breeze to disturb the tall coconut palms that stood baking in the sun. The big train puffed away in its clouds of steam, leaving the railroad station eerily deserted. I stood for a long time on the curb with my bags waiting for a taxi to cruise by. At last I saw one coming from far up the vacant avenue. I hailed it, tossed my suitcases onto the seat, and said, "Colonial Hotel."

"What's wrong with you, boy?" asked the driver. "What are you doing in Miami today?"

"I'm here on business," I said with a self-important air, "and I'm leaving in the morning for Jamaica."

"Don't bet on it, boy," my driver assured me as we rumbled along the steamy streets. "The worst hurricane you'll ever care to see is expected to strike in the morning."

There was very little traffic in Miami, and very little noise. But everywhere a strange hollow sound kept repeating its bang-bang-bang, echoing from near and far. The sound of hammering! Storm shutters were being nailed up all over town.

My hotel was an absolute bedlam. There was a general state of panic, and the intense heat didn't help any. Waves of humanity were storming the front desk, screaming for rooms. Fortunately, I had a reservation. There were babies, cats, dogs, and even crates of chickens strung out through the lobby, all wailing and barking and clucking at once. People had even brought pieces of furniture—chairs and tables—from their homes to save them from the impending holocaust; they had obviously seen Miami hurricanes before.

I made my way through the mob to my room. The first thing I did was fill the bathtub with water, as the desk clerk had instructed me to do, in case the water supplies were contaminated by the storm. I opened a window. The fireball sun, now low in the west, beat down relentlessly, and the stillness of the air was choking. I pushed once more through the throng in the lobby to the little airline office. There, I was assured that my flight would take off on schedule; the storm was going to pass to the east around noon, and I was heading south in the very early morning.

Back in my room, the telephone rang almost immediately.

"Come home at once," said Mrs. Wood. "Get on the midnight train if you have

63

*The dining room, with stenciled sailcloth curtains, a caprice of fringe tacked
to table and console shelf, iron chairs painted the color of bougainvillaea*

to, but get out of that city." I told her that I was flying out of the danger, and that she
needn't worry about me, but, in a voice mounting to the point of hysteria, she insisted
I return.

"Now, Mrs. Wood," I said, "I have come all this distance on a very uncomfortable
train, and the airlines have assured me I will be leaving long before the hurricane
strikes Miami. So please try not to worry." She pulled herself together and settled for
my promise that I would—if I could—send her a telegram from Kingston to assure
her I had arrived intact.

I realized I was very hungry. I took myself up to the rooftop restaurant, which
overlooked Biscayne Bay and would have been a spectacular place to eat had it not
been teeming with humanity. Everyone I had seen in the lobby was here, plus all their
relatives. It was an extraordinary scene: all the babies were crying, all the dogs were
barking, all the women were sobbing, and all the men were trying to drown their
problems in alcohol. I ate rather hurriedly in this excited atmosphere, went back to my
room, and slept surprisingly well, considering that all of Miami was preparing for its
doom.

The next day, I was out at the airport at the crack of dawn. I boarded an eleven-seater amphibious plane, only to discover that I was one of two passengers. All the rest had canceled, scared to death. My seat-mate was a traveling salesman (could I have had a better companion on a four-and-a-half-hour flight?) who talked nonstop and told me hair-raising tales of his other trips: how, once, his plane had been forced to land on an uncharted island, and all the passengers and crew risked being devoured by cannibals, et cetera. I was wide-eyed the whole trip, although the flight itself was uneventful. We stopped once to refuel in the harbor on the southern coast of Cuba at a lovely little town called Cienfuegos, which means "One Hundred Fires." It was my first landing on water, and a thrilling sensation. As we flew over Jamaica, the salesman told me that Port Arthur, a little town in the harbor, had sunk long ago and I eagerly strained my eyes, expecting to see rooftops sticking up from the water.

We landed at Kingston at about noon. As I was deplaning, a small, frail-looking man approached me. He had dark eyes and a smooth mauve complexion—obviously an East Indian. "Mr. Baldwin?" he said in a high, thin voice. He led me to his car—a doubtful-looking machine composed mainly of rust, and we began our long trip over the mountains to Montego Bay. This Hindu gentleman raced the car along the twisting, steep roads with admirable nonchalance, as I huddled tensely in the back seat, wondering if he knew what the brake pedal was for. The car clattered as if it would at any moment vibrate into a heap of scrap metal, and in my heart I knew it

Left, in the hall, tall doors, yellow as allamanda. Right, in the living room, one of a pair of trompe-l'oeil *commodes painted by Joseph B. Platt*

would never stand up to an impact at more than two miles an hour. The sight of oncoming trucks on this pitted and scarred road that passed for a highway filled me with terror, but my driver veered around and whizzed past them all at speeds well beyond the sound barrier, miraculously missing every one.

After a few hours of this, I decided it would be better for my health to look out the window. It was not hard to become absorbed in the strange and wonderful scenery. I had never before seen a banyan tree, and here were hundreds of the multitrunked wonders spreading over huge distances, with their aerial roots reaching down like loose threads at the hem of a great green garment. The flowers were fantastic—bougainvillaea and hibiscus and exotic bromeliads nestled in trees. We passed rain trees, aki trees, breadfruit trees, and plantations of pineapple and vanilla. Whenever we drove through a wretched little village, toothless old hags in shapeless dresses would rush at the car (he *had* to slow down then), shaking their fists at me and shouting "White son of a bitch, go away!" This in 1938!

We arrived in Montego Bay around eight o'clock—after eight solid hours on the road, and nearly thirteen of nonstop traveling—and pulled up to the Casa Blanca Hotel, an establishment that did not exactly strike me as a haven for the beleaguered traveler. I was at that point in a near-catatonic state, and could barely walk. And I was famished. I was handed a note at the desk that said I should expect to be called for in the morning by a Mr. Bond. When I asked about sending a telegram to Mrs. Wood, the desk clerk doubled up with laughter. I rushed to the dining room and was served an inedible bird purported to be a duck. I went to bed hungry and tired to the bone. My stomach rumbling, I fell grumpily asleep.

I awoke next morning to glorious sunshine and blazing heat. Outside my window was the Caribbean, deep and blue and inexpressibly beautiful. Right on the beach strutted macaws with flaming plumage of red and yellow and green, screeching for their breakfast at the tops of their little lungs. Somewhere in the hotel a Victrola was playing "Wabash Blues."

I pulled on my khaki shorts, packed a few things in a tiny bag, grabbed my portfolio, and went down to the dining room, where I was unable to eat, or even to identify, the breakfast. I opened the portfolio, which contained the plans of the house I was to see. The house had been designed by the brilliant architect Howard Major, of Palm Beach, and I looked forward to seeing it. This was to be the first really civilized dwelling in the mountains surrounding Montego Bay: a winter playhouse for a man and his wife, and all the guests they loved to have for weekends and holidays. There were to be lots of bathrooms and a swimming pool, and all sorts of other luxuries unheard of in the islands at that time.

Gradually, I became aware of a presence across my table, a tall, strikingly handsome black man dressed in a brilliant white shirt: Mr. Bond. It was a privilege to work with him: he was a Jamaican native who had been to Oxford; he carried himself erect and proud, and spoke in that lilting Jamaican accent I could listen to for hours. He was in charge of the over-all work of the house, including the supervision of all the workmen. He was, I could tell at a glance, the kind of man who took command of whatever situation he found himself in, and I knew I could trust him with anything.

We got into his car and drove up into the mountains where the house was being built. I was again impressed by the extraordinary vegetation of this island in the sun. It seemed to me that every leaf of every tree and bush was part of some great *chinoiserie*—unreal and almost too luxuriant. At the site itself, the building was well under way, and everything appeared to be running smoothly. The trestle table Bond had set up was piled with all his plans and business papers. The place was teeming with workmen. All around the site were little tents and wooden huts hastily erected by the men for their families, who had come to camp on the grounds while the work was being done.

Bond and I walked through the building together. The interior had not yet been plastered, but the walls were up and it was possible to visualize furniture arrangements. We spent the whole day discussing construction details and became so engrossed that we almost missed a glorious sunset. But then, the sky began to be overlaid with successively deeper shades of indigo, until finally it was like black silk, and overflowing with stars.

We ate a very good supper cooked on an open flame—the first solid meal I had had in twenty-four hours—and then Bond took me to a charming little tent that had been prepared for me. There was a satisfactory latrine nearby, a few big tubs of water from the spring up the mountainside, and a fire to heat the water for bathing. One of the workmen's wives offered to wash my shirt for me. I had an iron cot and a wonderful old oil lamp (as I knew I was not going to be reading much, its soft orange light was perfectly adequate). I sat in my tent looking over the plans Bond and I had worked on that day, and I gradually began to be aware that I was not alone. My heart racing in my chest, I looked cautiously around. Under the folds of my tent were dozens of bright little eyes peering up at me: children (and even some grownups) stealing this quiet moment to investigate the strange creature who was suddenly among them. I snuffed out my light and went to sleep, feeling safe and snug.

For the next four or five days, we worked on correcting the few details Bond had misunderstood; he had supervised most of the work perfectly well. One thing that was to him unfathomable was the plan that called for a bathroom with every bedroom. Another piece of Yankee illogic was the presence of a fireplace: who ever heard of a fireplace in the tropics? But Bond had made some innovative improvements on the plans as drawn, and had proudly approved the interior plaster himself. The workmen were enormously pleased with themselves, and loved to hear Bond and me praise them.

A guest room with beds that belong on a carrousel, swagged with pink mosquito netting and spread with roses stenciled in candy pink

More stenciling in the living room: bright-yellow orchids on the armless chairs. Bicolorous window valances are white on the inside, yellow on the outside.

They worked from just after dawn until sundown, taking a nice long siesta in the hottest part of the day, just after lunch. Everyone was laughing and happy all the time, by which I knew perfectly well I wasn't in New York.

On the third morning, Bond came up to me as I was shaving under a tree. "I know you must be quite bored living up here all this time," he said with a smile. "I have some business in town, and I want you to come down for a holiday."

He drove me through the little markets of Montego Bay, and smiled to see how excited I was. I felt like a child at a birthday party. Everywhere were women with huge baskets on their heads, hawking their wares. There were wonderful, curious-looking fruits I had never seen, and some I had never even heard of: star apples and aki and breadfruit and papaya. In one section of the market, piles of beautiful cotton-madras plaids gleamed purple, red, green, yellow, and marvelous earth-brown. I learned later that they had been made in India, bought by England, and sent to Jamaica. I was so delighted by the madras that I bought yards of it to make into summer slip covers for my little white apartment on Sutton Place. (I also had some swimming trunks done up, and later made a very good impression on a host when I dove into his pool and left a rainbow of dyes all through the water behind me.)

"Now, Mr. Baldwin," said my companion in his lyrical, low voice, "I am going to take you to see a lady who has a salon, where every afternoon, the mayor, the best lawyer in Montego Bay, the best doctor, and the head judge of the court gather to talk over the affairs of the town."

I climbed eagerly into the car and we drove up to a gate in a huge wall. We got out and walked through. There was a vivid-green lawn and a riot of hibiscus, much bigger and more varied in color than any I had seen before. As for the bougainvillaea, there were fountains and curtains and fireworks of it, in incredible paradise colors of magenta and salmon and brilliant raspberry pink.

As we walked along, I became aware of a peculiar sound—a soft hum, like the buzzing of a million bees. Bond, smiling, led me to a building nearby and told me to look in at the glassless window. The sound was coming from Chinese children in a kindergarten reciting their lessons with their teacher. I had not realized that there was a sizable Chinese population in Jamaica.

The main house was an impressive building painted butter yellow and surrounded by jungly growth. The house was built slightly into the hillside, so that even though the entrance was on the ground floor, the windows on the opposite side of the entrance hall rose from sills on a level with the grass outside. Little balconies of iron grillwork looped around each window, and luxuriant beds of maidenhair fern trailed over into the room. Because it was sunk partially into the earth like that, the room felt wonderfully cool and refreshing.

We were taken upstairs into the main rooms of the house, where we saw four or five men, very tall, their smooth black faces and hands a startling contrast to their brilliant white shirts: the elders of the town, including the mayor himself. They were all full of questions about me, my work, and the people who would be moving into the house. We had all set to talking very animatedly when suddenly there was a hush, and all eyes turned toward the stairs.

Down the mahogany staircase, her hand gliding gracefully along the polished banister, came Madame, her skin the color of pale honey. She put me instantly in mind of Napoleon's Josephine, who was a beautiful Creole from Martinique. Madame was not so much fat as very ample. Her dark hair was piled in clusters on top of her head, except for two great curls that corkscrewed around her ears. She spoke with a charming Jamaican accent in a voice that sounded like music, and her twinkling eyes were brilliant green.

She wore a most unusual dress: fresh cotton the color of pink coral, with a broad V-shaped opening in front that extended from her shoulders to well below her waist. Into this opening, Madame had inserted tiers of folded pink Kleenex, row upon row, like ruffles, filling the entire décolletage. I considered the time she must have spent arranging them. I saw her pull out the topmost tissue and, with an elegant gesture, wipe the dewdrops of perspiration from her brow. She then dropped the tissue into a nearby basket. She repeated this performance from time to time throughout the afternoon. By the end of the visit, she was totally naked from the waist up.

Bond and I left this remarkable gathering and motored back to the house in great good humor. We were immediately confronted with the problem of the day: how to camouflage the water tank (there had to be one because of the difficulties in transporting water up to the middle of the mountain). We finally decided to dig the huge tank into the hillside that sloped away from the house, cover it with soil, and plant a garden on top of it. We later installed a swimming pool at the foot of the tank, which was camouflaged with a row of tall pepper trees, their roots at swimming-pool level, their tops on a line with the house.

Slowly, the decoration began to take shape in my mind. Mrs. Wood and I had thought it should be almost in the spirit of a ballet, whimsical and light and sketchy. There could be almost no wood at all because of termites and other tiny, omnivorous beasts. What had to be wood would be mahogany, a hard native tree that did not seem to agree with the termites' delicate stomachs. The rest would be metal. In most of the bedrooms, for instance, the chests of drawers were made of metal with baked enamel finishes, some painted to match the cottons in the room. There were two bedrooms done just alike in polka dots, one in black and white, the other in red and white, with their little chests polka-dotted to match. In some rooms, the chests were painted by Joseph B. Platt in *trompe-l'oeil* and were very chic indeed.

It was obvious what colors we would be using. I could envision those plaster-white walls with nothing else but the strong bright colors of the fabulous flowers that filled the countryside. The house itself would be a white flower amid the green of the surrounding vegetation. And the only fabric allowed would be cotton, from the sheerest voile to the heaviest canvas. Mrs. Wood and I later decided that it would be fun to have some of the fabrics specially printed. She and her brother-in-law, Harry Cimino, designed a series of stenciled fabrics: one, I remember, was a flat pink rose stenciled on heavy white canvas; another was a highly stylized bougainvillaea in its own natural ruby color.

The room that was most fun to decorate was the big guest dormitory, for bachelors and sons of the family, above the garage. Alternating with six huge windows—three on each side—were six single, iron four-posters. We based the decoration on a fashion drawing by Christian Bérard: each bed had a canopy of a different warm, strong color—pink, yellow, magenta, or lilac—with white ball fringe and bedspreads to match. Each bed had its own bedside table and lamp on one side, and a washstand with pitcher, bowl, and wall mirror on the other (there were also two complete bathrooms, one at each end of the room). The tray ceiling was high, for coolness, and the cross-ventilation from the big windows kept a pleasant light breeze wafting through at almost any hour of the day or night. It looked like a carnival, with nothing missing but balloons.

The one exception to the house's white-and-flowers motif was the library, a perfectly square room, which we paneled with pecky cypress, an attractive pale wood from Florida. The sofa and chairs we covered in a beige cotton felt that had been immunized against humidity. In the center of the room was a big desk where the owner could work during his holidays. It was to this room that the gardeners and other employees of the household would come barefoot, lining up out in the hall to receive their salaries on payday. The only decorative thing in the room was an amusing circular rug, a huge compass made of appliquéd felt in beige, black, and emerald green, aligned, of course, with the magnetic north.

My work was finished, and I left the site in high spirits, with everything planned on paper and vivid in my mind's eye. I couldn't wait to get back to Mrs. Wood with my ideas. This time, Bond drove me. It was not as thrilling a drive as the first one, but it was just as scenic—through a wonderful old plantation and some delightful little towns to the Kingston airport.

I arrived in Miami to learn two pieces of big news: appeasement had been reached in Europe, and the hurricane had missed Miami completely. Not even a slight breeze had been felt. It had, instead, devastated Long Island, where Mrs. Wood had implored me to come for refuge. While I had been living my Jamaican fantasy, Mrs. Wood's property in Syosset had been laid to waste; forty trees that had lived for a hundred years were utterly destroyed by the great hurricane of '38.

CHAPTER 7

Take a
Room

A LECTURE TO THE STUDENTS OF THE
PARSONS SCHOOL OF DESIGN IN NEW YORK, 1950

A DECORATOR'S WORK is essentially domestic. It is not work with stage sets or display windows. It is private, not public. The human element counts most of all. "How do you plan to use this room?" I first ask any client, for suitability is the most important element in any decoration. A decorator must consider the kind of people for whom he works, how they live, and their stated budget. Then, and only then, can he execute their wishes and requirements according to the best of his trained taste and experience.

Next to suitability, restraint is the most important quality. If a decorator follows these two commandments, he has more than half won the fight for a successful fundamental background. Decorators must create comfortable, workable, and *restrained* settings for the personal memorabilia of their clients.

Here, I have taken an actual case, chosen to show how to decorate a specific room in a specific house to serve people with specific interests and tastes.

The Place

A converted stable on the property of a large house. The owners' children have all grown up and moved away. The big house can no longer be maintained at its proper level, and the owners prefer to change entirely their scale of life, remodel the stable, and move into it.

The Room

Twenty feet wide, thirty feet long, it has only an eight-and-one-half-foot ceiling broken by rough beams. It must serve as a combination living room, dining room, and library. Primarily for summer living, the house (which has heating facilities) will often be used for winter weekends. Most of the furnishings have been saved from the big house.

The People

The couple who own this converted stable lead quiet lives and care for the harmony of comfort and beauty. From the big house, they bring with them a few of

73

their favorite pieces in a collection of furniture of all kinds and nationalities, antique and modern. They have traveled extensively, bought everywhere, fortunately with great discrimination and care. Their taste is catholic, their point of view broad. This shows in the paintings they own as well as in the furniture. The husband collects first-rate contemporary paintings and drawings, bright, gay, and personal. His wife has a charming garden. A little greenhouse opens off the living room and the house will be filled with fresh flowers even in winter.

The Specifications

The ground-floor plan of the converted stable consists of one large room, as we already know, plus a kitchen, servant's room, and bath. On the second floor are two double bedrooms and baths. The house cannot comfortably accommodate more than four people. Immediately, this suggests permanent dining arrangements for four in the large room, at a table that can seat six if necessary. Buffet service will take care of larger parties.

The "living" aspect of the room clearly calls for comfortable sofas and chairs with good reading lights and convenient smoking tables for four. As the owners are agents for playwrights, they often read scripts aloud. They need adequate space for books—on shelves and scattered about on tables. Also, they often play canasta or bridge. In addition, they own a Magnavox and a collection of excellent records. Convenient storage space for albums must be considered.

Although in this country house much of the life will go on out of doors, in cold

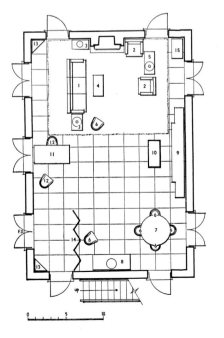

1. sofa
2. upholstered chair
3. two tables with lamps
4. coffee table
5. table with lamp
6. six Louis XVI armchairs
7. round dining table
8. commode
9. breakfront
10. metal table
11. writing table
12. pair of chairs
13. pair of corner cabinets
14. screen
15. record player

rainy weather the room will take the place of terrace or garden. It must be cheerful and gay.

Our clients have not an unlimited budget. As a matter of fact, this simple house would not be suitably decorated in an elaborate or expensive way. Here, we use restraint financially as well as artistically.

The Answer

A restrained background of floor, walls, ceiling, and curtains can substitute for and enormously help the awkward architectural proportions created by the low ceiling. This is a particularly useful device for the oddly proportioned rooms built in current New York apartment houses.

The room plan shows five French windows and four wooden doors. (One of the French windows doubles as entrance, or front door, of the house.) I know at once that the walls and curtains must be the same color; it would be a grave error to have the two long walls split by lengths of contrasting color in the curtains. As the ceiling is only eight feet six inches high, division by color would emphasize the lack of height. I plan the curtains to hang full, straight from the top of the window trim to the floor. Valances would only lower the height of the room to the eye. The curtains will draw; all curtains should draw—they are meant to shut out the darkness of night and to establish privacy. If clients do not care about these two elements, I see no reason to have curtains.

To give further illusion of height to the room, the ceiling and beams should be painted a slightly lighter shade than the walls. I am not now considering specific colors, but only what, for the sake of atmosphere and proportion, should be light and what should be dark in tone. *Deciding the actual color nearly always comes last, since the shape of the room itself and the furniture arrangement make up the structure of the room. Color is like icing on a cake. I never begin with a "color scheme."*

Finally, we come to the floor, which is the foundation of the room. I insist that floors be the same color as walls, only darker, to make a base. Beautiful floor tiles, made to order in any color, can be bought inexpensively and laid in any arrangement. We choose large squares in two tones of the same color. Since this is primarily a summer house, rugs are not essential. For the winter months, when it is pleasant to sit with one's feet on a covered floor, we can place an antique needlework or a contemporary rug to take in the fireplace group.

Now the room moves from its dark floor shade up into a medium shade for walls, woodwork, and curtains, and on to a light shade to help lift the beamed ceiling. This use of shades of one color gives a serenity and architectural calm that contrasting colors would never achieve. *Decorators should increase good proportion when it exists and endeavor to supply it by color and scale when it does not.*

The next step is placing the furniture. We start with the pieces the clients have and want to use. *Decorators should never insist on throwing out everything the client has. Even when they are far from perfect, loved possessions add personality.*

From a little, seldom-used drawing room of the big house comes a set of six Louis XVI medallion-backed armchairs in brocade. In the same room with these beautiful, comfortable chairs were also two Louis XVI square-backed side chairs covered in a dull stripe, and a fine twelve-foot bookcase of the same period. All of this furniture is finished in the original white paint.

We insist that the new upholstered furniture we have to buy be of the best quality. Starting with the fireplace, or sitting, group (on the furniture plan) we need a seven-foot sofa, long, low, and extremely comfortable. For the opposite side of the hearth, we buy two large upholstered chairs. These provide four seats for reading or relaxing that look and are luxuriously comfortable. The three pieces are upholstered in a neutral-colored sateen, ready for slip covers. Furniture upholstered in a simple sateen looks respectable even when the slip covers are at the cleaners. The large sofa takes a slip cover of the same fabric as the curtains, whatever we decide on. In a contrasting color, this great mass would get out of hand, look twice as large as it already is, and devour the room. *Large immovable furniture should be quietly permanent. "Floating" chairs can be as brilliant as one wishes.* The two upholstered chairs will have slip covers of patterned cloth. This breaks the so far unpatterned scheme.

Two tables, preferably Louis XVI mahogany pieces, must be bought for each end of the sofa, the one by the wall rather small, the one out in the room larger, to hold lamps and to accommodate books and flowers as well. A low, modern smoking table, with legs and top completely covered in pigskin leather, bought by the owners in Paris from the late Jean-Michel Frank, can be used in front of the sofa. The big house offers up a beautiful black Louis XV table, with the simplest of curved legs and no carving or ornamentation except bold ormolu hardware. This finishes a comfortable sitting group around the fireplace, which has a classic Louis XVI marble mantel from the big house.

Now for the six Louis XVI armchairs. Four of these are permanently well placed around the dining table. One joins the sitting group at the end of the sofa, where it acts as seasoning in its bright new covering. The sixth chair stands against the north wall, at the dining end of the room.

The important missing link in the furniture is a dining table. This must serve two purposes—the obvious one of eating, and, with a felt cover, card playing. It should also be practical for bottles and glasses and the necessities of a cocktail party. After much searching, we settle on a round Louis XVI mahogany table, three feet in diameter, with a pale marble top. With the addition of a separate folding top four feet in diameter, six chairs can be drawn up to this table.

On the north wall, opposite the fireplace, there is an eight-foot space between the door to the inside staircase and the pantry door. Here we place a four-foot commode to hold silver, playing cards, bridge and tea cloths, napkins, et cetera. This commode is a simple Italian Louis XV one, painted in grays and beiges with black lines.

Obviously, the only spot for the French bookcase from the big house is along the sixteen-foot space between the windows on the west wall. Books fill the top section of this handsome piece of furniture, and record albums occupy the bottom cupboards. A modern table, brass and glass, stands about a foot away from the bookcase and directly in front of it to hold albums taken out while records are being played.

The owners also want a desk in the room. To fill this need, we buy an Italian Directoire table, five feet by two feet six inches. This is placed in front of the middle window on the east wall and flanked by the two Louis XVI side chairs from the big house, reupholstered in the same fabric as the medallion-backed chairs.

From the hall of the big house come two English Regency mahogany commodes for the southeast and northeast corners of the room.

Remember that one of the French windows is the entrance, or front door, of the house. To overcome this defect, a seven-foot, six-fold screen forms a sort of wall reaching out at right angles from the north wall and placed just beyond the door to the staircase. But a tall screen cuts out light and certainly obliterates crosslight in this end of the room. To beat this problem, we designed a screen with six panels eighteen inches wide, each of opaque glass framed by wood painted the wall color.

This brings us squarely up to the important question of lighting. The three tables in the sitting group all take lamps. These should have both direct and indirect fixtures. The writing table allows plenty of room for a small lamp. On the commode in the northeast corner stands a lamp to light the improvised vestibule. A large lamp will go on the painted commode to light the table while it is being set or when it is being cleared off. On the west wall at each end, there will be wall brackets. All these lamps should have simple modern forms in black or white, and should not be overpoweringly large. There is one exception: an antique Louis XVI *bouillotte* from the drawing room of the big house. All the shades are off-white painted paper. *The insides of such shades should be tinted pale pink to kill hard, unbecoming light. Covering the tops of the shades with paper avoids spots of light on ceiling and walls.*

Over the fireplace goes a gilt-framed Louis XVI mirror the width of the mantel and hung so that it rests on it, with the top almost touching the ceiling. Over the commode on the north wall, with its eight-foot space between the staircase and pantry door, hangs the largest painting. On the east wall are two six-foot spaces at either side of the middle window, good spots for pictures. With walls and curtains the same color, paintings do not have to compete with them in pattern or color. *An uncluttered background never results in monotony or dullness; it creates calmness and serenity, and brings out the best in good furniture. I recommend a dark color scheme for bad furniture and a light scheme for good furniture. By dark, I never mean dull—I mean brilliantly dark. In most cases, curtains should not be a focal point of a room. It is best for them to be a part of the background.*

Now, and only now, do we choose the color scheme of the room. A pinky-beige linen for the curtains and the large sofa. The covering on the French chairs, a brilliant-yellow domestic silk-and-cotton mixture. The slip covers for the two upholstered chairs are a printed cotton.

As a fundamental of good decoration, I always advise my clients to buy the best they can afford, antique or modern, and to leave a space empty if necessary until it can be filled by something of real value. I avoid the sensational in any type of fabric or furniture unless there is unlimited money, allowing for frequent changes. Too often the novelty of today is the bad taste of tomorrow. Nothing will last whose only virtue is that it is "different."

Decorators should provide a serene, uncluttered background for people, pictures, flowers, books, and the unavoidable and necessary confusion brought into a room by living. All rooms should grow after decorators leave them, and good decorators should allow room for growth.

It is wrong to *impose* taste; we must *interpret* the client's taste and wishes. Any house or room remembered with pleasure has the look of being loved by those who live in it. I will go so far as to say that I prefer an ugly, personal room to one that is just cold and correct—a mausoleum done by a decorator.

Here, in a couple of short paragraphs, is the best bible for decorators that I know of, an excerpt from Rue W. Carpenter's *Problems in Decoration*.

"The effectiveness of any given example of interior decoration is based primarily on what it achieves in point of 'suitability.' This element of suitability must take into account the environment, the utilitarian purpose of the building as a whole or of the room to be treated, and also in some degree the character and type of the occupant, to say nothing of the financial budget on which the work may be based.

"The decorator must face his task with no rules or formulas to guide him; he must depend upon his own sense of suitability and proportion and his feeling for color and form. At the very outset, he must deny himself the convenient luxury of a personal style or a favorite 'period' and all predilections of color and arrangement, and he must substitute for these a purely objective point of view. He must then discard his own fear of mistakes. Otherwise, he handicaps himself with a fatal self-consciousness that will force him in self-defence to accept mere 'correctness' as his objective. In a word, the mood of his approach to his task should be a happy mixture of fearlessness and common sense and that priceless ingredient, artistic ingenuity."

CHAPTER 8

El Señor Puerco: Pre-Castro Cuba, 1957

HAVANA WAS A CITY I had caught only glimpses of on my way back and forth to Mexico, and it was dazzling (part of the appeal, I'm sure, had something to do with that indescribable Cuban daiquiri, which still lingers in my memory). So when I was offered the chance to decorate the hacienda on a small sugar plantation, I jumped at it.

The plantation was owned by El Señor Puerco, a Venezuelan by birth who now controlled a staggering proportion of the world's sugar. I had met the *señor* once, at a party given by a mutual friend of ours, a woman of taste and great decorating experience. Puerco had asked her to do his house, but she had insisted upon my professional assistance. Puerco was short and stocky, with a disproportionately large head, bald except for a scraggle of gray hair. His eyes were glinting and black, like shot, and his face, although it could break into a rather attractive smile, was all steely shrewdness. He wore no jewelry on his huge, capable hands, but the nails were polished to a degree.

The house was to be for the bride the *señor* was about to take, a European of quite celebrated ill repute. Puerco's children had publicly vowed never to speak to their father again if he married the woman. But marry her he did, and now my friend and I were to decorate all the rooms except hers, which she preferred to do herself. We were practically given carte blanche; Puerco told us how he would be using the hacienda, and sent the floor plan and some photographs of the elevations. We arranged the furniture from the plan (I knew I would probably be making a few changes once I saw the actual rooms), found all the furniture and materials, and I drew up my estimates, carefully itemizing everything and listing valuations for insurance purposes.

Since the house was in the tropics, it was to be rather bare, with a great deal of iron and wicker furniture and, thanks to the termite problem, very little wood. (Several years before, Mrs. Wood had done a house in Havana that called for a mirrored dressing table. When the owners—who lived in the house all winter and closed it for the summer—returned the following season they found not a dressing table, but a pile of shattered mirrors: the bugs had devoured the entire wood frame. That was my lesson about termites.) We planned also to use cotton and linen absolutely everywhere. I remember particularly a smashing black-and-white design for the front hall. The *señor* signed and approved everything; it was all going smooth as, well, cotton!

My friend had told me privately that the *señor*'s taste was dreadful. She advised me to fill the walls with simple drawings and water colors so there would be no room for the kind of pictures *he* was likely to put up. I could not even conceive of keeping a client from having pictures he liked on his own walls; yet my friend was usually right about other people's taste. In any case, the house had very little wall space because of all the wonderful windows in the plan, and the mirrors I had already decided to use. But I ordered the drawings anyway.

August came. New York was stifling; Havana was reporting 102° in the shade. One week before the crates of furniture were scheduled to arrive in Cuba, I received a telephone call from El Puerco's secretary, an efficient, demanding woman who told me in a strident voice that everyone was waiting impatiently for the shipment, although she knew perfectly well it was not due for a week. I was to bring work clothes, because I would be working, not socializing. At least I knew where I stood.

A week later I was ready to go. I had the shipping lists and my little suitcase with overalls and a toothbrush. I prayed that everything had gotten to Havana all right. We had taken care not only of the rugs and furniture and fabrics, but also of the china, silver, linen, even the soap—everything for the complete installation of the house. I had been bluntly informed that everything would have to be completed in a single day. I was to stay at El Puerco's Havana house, and whatever misgivings I may have had about that were mitigated somewhat by the news that he had the finest cuisine in all Havana. "You're in for a treat," said my friend. "El Puerco's food is worth a day of his atrocious manners and awful taste."

Standing in the ticket line at the airport, I felt a tug at my elbow. I looked around. Nobody. I looked down. There stood a tiny little man, dressed all in black, with huge, opaque black sunglasses above a brush of a mustache. I was put in mind of the dwarfs in Velásquez's paintings.

"I know you are Mr. Baldwin," said the little man in a thick Spanish accent. "There will be a package on the airplane with you. You will not know what is in it. It is for Sr. Puerco. When you arrive in Havana, you will check with the stewardess to be sure the package has been taken care of."

Without waiting for a response, he turned abruptly and disappeared into the milling crowds. Well, I thought, a bit of high adventure. I wondered whether the package contained narcotics or jewels. And what if I were questioned? What would government officials think when I told them that it was a dwarf in dark glasses who was responsible for my traveling with contraband goods? By the time we arrived in Havana, I had half decided to pretend ignorance. But my curiosity got the best of me.

"Do you happen to know . . . ?" I asked the stewardess rather hesitantly. "There is supposed to be a package . . ."

"Oh, yes, Mr. Baldwin," she interrupted, grinning broadly. "It has been taken care of." I wondered even more what on earth it could be—so closely followed, so well concealed, yet so blatantly acknowledged.

I stepped out of the plane into the blast of a furnace; not even a New Yorker could imagine heat like this. I was walking away from the plane gasping for air when two gigantic hulks of men, both black, scowling, and wearing huge black raincoats, took my mind off the heat. They were approaching me with looks of unrelenting determination, and just as I was about to go through the customs line, they jerked my bags out of my hands. But instead of taking me through customs or, worse, into the customs office itself, they escorted me in solemn silence to a huge gray limousine and drove off with me across the city.

Outside my tank of a car, Havana was blazing with color and greenery. The frangipani was blooming in huge pink clusters; there were riots of hibiscus and bougainvillaea; and the fantastic *flamboyants* were weighed down so heavily by their red-orange clusters of flowers that their branches nearly brushed the ground. Here was the Havana I remembered from long ago.

The great car drew to a stop in front of a big, dark house, and one of the two enormous Cubans got out.

"We are now at the *señor's* house," he said in businesslike tones. "You will be waited on by the houseman, who speaks no English." He pounded on the door with a fist the size of a leg of lamb and left me in the care of a frail-looking, dark-complexioned man in a baggy white jacket.

I stepped eagerly into the darkness of the house and out of the intolerable Havana heat, and thought I would die on the spot of frostbite. The air conditioning was so intense I was literally chilled to the bone. I began shivering uncontrollably. My little houseman apparently did not notice. He trotted smilingly along before me to my room, a dark but comfortable-looking chamber with a white marble floor, white rugs, and terrible, ugly, dark pictures all over the walls. We reached an agreement by rather complicated sign language that dinner was to be at eight o'clock and that I was not to dress. As soon as he left, I rushed to the window and threw open the shutters. The inrushing hot air mingling with the intense cold of my room produced a bit of fog, but at least the temperature was now tolerable. I took a shower, organized my things, and, as my host had not yet appeared, decided to take a little stroll around the house.

It is not possible to exaggerate the hideousness of that house. The shutters were closed against the heat, and as a consequence there was almost no light. When my eyes adjusted to the gloom, I could see that the rooms were filled with the most awful reproduction French furniture, mostly Louis XIV and XV, all glistening ostentatiously and covered with flashy new brocade. I noticed, however, that the furniture was made by someone who knew at least how to carve—the craftsmanship was excellent. On the walls were the most ghastly reproductions of the great old masters, all done in thick oil paint. My friend was right; I was glad for the water colors I had brought.

At a pair of big doors, I knocked, listened, and, hearing no sound, opened them and went in. I found myself in an oval room done completely in the style of Napoleon: Empire paneling and shining new reproduction furniture and, in the center of the room, a large round table upon which sat a bronze death mask of Napoleon himself. I went over to touch it and my fingers nearly stuck to the freezing metal.

I got out of that room fast and headed down another long corridor. I seemed to be alone in the house. The houseman must have been seeing to dinner; where my host was I had no idea. I spied a bit of light at the end of the hall and was drawn toward it like a moth. Its source was a long veranda filled with lovely plants and hideous furniture. Beyond was a swimming pool of turquoise water that seemed to be sending up clouds of steam. I watched, fascinated, wondering if the pool were going to boil over. Then I took a turn down another dark passageway, only to be confronted by another pair of double doors. I knocked, listened, and knocked again. There was a low growl. I opened the doors hesitantly.

The room was in darkness except for a lamp standing on a desk in the center of the room and shining only on the desk, leaving everything else, including the face of the person seated there, totally obscured. I assumed, however, that this must be El Señor Puerco. He said nothing, so I cleared my throat and began:

"Good afternoon, sir."

"What?" he greeted me, ever the gracious host. "What is this?"

"I'm Billy Baldwin," I said—perhaps he didn't remember?—"and I've come . . ."

"Oh, yes, yes," he said. "Sit down."

I felt my way across the pitch-black room to a peculiar-looking chair. It turned out to be one of those reclining lounge chairs and I landed in a horizontal position with my feet practically in the señor's face—a rather attractive beginning, I thought. The granite face was not disturbed by so much as a wrinkle of a smile; it calmly waited as I hastily righted myself and mustered my most pleasant expression.

"Very nice to see you," he recited. "Dinner will be at eight, and I will meet you in the solarium. My chef is in Paris, so don't expect anything grand." I couldn't hide my disappointment—it was the food that was to make this whole trip worthwhile! Oh, well, I thought, even if it's not roast pheasant, it will be very nice. "We must get up very early in the morning, so after we eat we'll go straight to bed," he continued. "I expect you to have everything done by tomorrow evening. We'll get you to the house by seven thirty and you can just work until you're through."

"I really do hope everything has arrived, and that all the tools are there," I said. "Setting up an entire household is a gigantic task. What if we run into difficulties?"

"You *will* get it done," he said flatly. "There will be *no* difficulties. You will have plenty of slaves to help you. Now go along and get cleaned up and meet me at eight." He directed his attention to the papers on his desk and did not look up again. I was able to figure out for myself that the interview was over; I rose with great care from that dangerous chair, and tiptoed out the door.

At one minute to eight, I set forth for the solarium. There I found the *señor* with a very pretty girl of eighteen or twenty and a tall young man in a snow-white suit. Sr.

Puerco introduced me to his daughter (I wondered where she had come from—had she been in the house while I was wandering around it alone?), and then grinned slyly. "You see this bird here?" he said (apparently they did not speak English). "He is the leading painter of the Cuban school, of which there is none. He thinks he is going to get my daughter, but he is not." Presently, the two young people left, and the little houseman brought delicious daiquiris.

We then sat down at the table and out of the kitchen came a large platter upon which lay a chicken, cut in half, broiled, and mounted on a pile of mashed potatoes surrounded by canned peas and carrots. I took my half of the chicken and some vegetables, but the *señor* took nothing at all; he just sat and watched me eat. I was then given some very good Cuban coffee and sent to bed.

I was called at 5:00 A.M. and guided, bleary-eyed, to that huge gray car in which sat the chauffeur and a young man who I somehow felt was one of El Puerco's illegitimate children (I had been told that there were many!). The sun had not yet risen, but it already felt like noon in July in New York, and I knew the day was going to be a scorcher. The chauffeur drove wildly, hit several chickens, and narrowly missed some small children playing well off the side of the road. After two harrowing hours, we arrived at the plantation.

"I will be back to fetch you promptly at seven," said my driver, revving the motor. And away he pulled, leaving me alone in front of this strange hacienda, with a full day stretching before me. I heaved a sigh and went in.

The house was beautiful, quite modern with some Spanish influence; a broad terrace swung around on three sides, and there was a wonderful pool and marvelous trees perfectly placed by the architect. The house was complete, but it was also empty. There was a large entrance hall, which we had decided to furnish as part of the living room, a sort of library-sitting room combination, a dining room, several guest bedrooms, and the master's bedroom itself. The walls were white; the floors white marble, and the windows huge and gloriously open to the sky. What a contrast to his city house!

In the entrance hall to greet me was an enormous pile of crates, still nailed shut— and a group of men, eight of them, ranging in age from about fourteen to at least eighty: my slaves. A strong-looking young man stepped boldly up to me as his colleagues hung back, shy and smiling.

"I speak English," he said clearly. "I only."

"That's perfectly wonderful," I said. "That's all we need."

"No understand," said the boy with a look of smiling bewilderment. "I can say 'New York,' 'yes,' and 'no.'"

Now I understood all too well. Here we were, with tons of furniture and china and soap to be put around the house within a matter of hours, no means of communication, and everyone smiling. It was a terrific start.

Well, we might as well get going, I thought to myself. I snatched up a crowbar lying nearby and began prying open one of the crates. There was a great roar of laughter from the men as they all found crowbars and began tearing into the crates. They copied every move I made, and never stopped laughing all day. It was like some kind of ballet; I would swing a wicker chair up over my head and go running up the marble steps; instantly, eight laughing Cubans would whisk their chairs over their heads and run right along behind me. Thus was the entire house assembled, and it went like magic, all accomplished with smiles.

Toward noon, I saw a shadow hovering in the background. A young woman of extraordinary beauty, thirty at the most, with the saddest expression I had ever seen, walked silently across the bare floor to me and said, in a lovely, low, hushed voice, a single word: "Lunch." As if by prearranged signal, everyone else vanished. I thought at first that the lovely creature was in rags, but it was just her sweet Cinderella sadness that gave that impression; she was actually wearing a little dress of faded violet-colored cotton. She put up a card table and brought a little chair for me to sit on. She poured a glass of local wine and then brought in, on a tray, a lunch consisting of a huge loaf of bread with either an animal or a fowl inside—it was impossible to determine which; or it might just as easily have been shoe leather, judging by its texture and taste. I considered for a moment the consequences of eating it, but then I felt so sorry for the charming girl who had gone to all the trouble of preparing it for me, and who stood watching so appealingly from a distance, that I ate as much of it as I could. For dessert, there was a sort of candy made of sweet potatoes. The wine was really very good.

Without warning, there came a terrific flash of light, and then a thunderbolt so alarming that I jerked several inches off my chair. Lightning and thunder crashed all around the house, and deafening rain poured down in sheets as thick as glass. I sat, trembling and terrified and totally alone, in an empty white room at a little white table, trying to eat a shoe-leather sandwich in the midst of an electrical storm that might end my life at any second.

Almost as suddenly as it had come up, the storm died away, leaving the sun no less scorching and the land incredibly no less dry than they had been before. Not even the air had been cooled by the torrent. I put down my napkin and stood up. Instantly, everyone appeared; the table was taken away, and life with my slaves resumed.

We uncrated and arranged the furniture, hung the pictures, put away all the china and glass and silver. The total breakage was two glasses. By the end of the day, we were all exhausted, and sweat was pouring off bodies, but we had everything done. The men were beaming with pride.

At about six o'clock, I heard a familiar roar outside by the gate. It was the big gray car with the chauffeur and the quasi son come to fetch me. I told the son I wanted to give each of my helpers something for the wonderful job they had done.

"You must be mad," he said. "You can beat them if they don't work, but give them something? Never." (If I had ever doubted that this boy was spawned by El Puerco, I doubted no longer.)

"Of course I will give them something," I insisted, "and I would like you to suggest a sum that is not too small, nor so big that they are likely to think of me as some fat cat from America." The boy could not bring himself to help me. So I chose a sum myself, and marched back into the house to give it to each workman, including the two frail old men, who were so tired and bent they could barely lift the teaspoons by the end of the day. To a man, they wept. It was obviously the first time in their lives that they had been thanked for anything.

I went back to the car. "I would also like to give something to that charming young woman who served me my lunch," I said.

"Oh, you can't give anything to her," said the young man, laughing hideously as he nudged me into the car. "She is the *señor*'s former mistress, recently given the boot, and is to be the maid of the incoming bride." The thought almost turned my stomach.

In the back seat of the car, I discovered another passenger—a large, white-haired man with a very comfortable-looking stomach indeed. He was settled contentedly in the opposite corner, smiling and holding in one large paw a smoldering Havana cigar. He wore a dark-blue alpaca suit, a pale-blue shirt, and a gleaming-white Panama hat. His eyes were brilliant blue and his expression the most pleasant and intelligent I had encountered thus far in Cuba. He did not introduce himself.

"I have seen the house," he told me in a thick, charming accent, though I had certainly not seen him anywhere about, "and you have done a very good job. I hope Sr. Puerco appreciates it; he has not got one drop of taste in his blood vessel." He went on in great detail, very wittily, about the taste of his friend, and, in spite of the terrific heat and fearful driving, I was able to relax on the long trip home. He spoke with pride of Cuba's culture, future, and brand-new oil industry. Cuba, he said, was going to be a wonderful place. Two years later, Castro came to power.

When we arrived at the house, my new friend said he would not be coming in. I wondered who he was and I hoped I would see him again. In my room, I found a note from El Puerco: "I have gone to a party at the American Embassy, which wouldn't interest you at all. If you have done the job as it was supposed to be done, you are probably very tired. Go to bed early because you will be called at seven."

I took an hourlong shower, put on a nice clean pair of pants and a white shirt, and walked through the gloom of the frigid hall to the solarium. I just knew I would catch pneumonia the instant I landed in New York. I was cheered up by the sight of the little houseman holding in two hands a silver cocktail shaker taller than he was. I sat down and closed my eyes and let the delectable nectar trickle over my taste buds. Then what should appear from the kitchen but *the* platter from the night before, containing the other half of the chicken and the rest of the uneaten canned vegetables. I did not even have to look closely to see in the potatoes the imprint of the chicken I had had the night before. The whole platter was only barely warmed, and the potatoes were a sodden mass. That was my second and final meal at the house of the man who served the finest food in Havana.

I managed to get down a couple of bites, concentrating on my daiquiris, and retired as quickly as I could to my room.

The next morning I was called at seven, as promised. I was led upstairs to a part of the house I had not yet seen, and taken into a sort of tower room with a spectacular view of the harbor. There, already dressed for the day, stood El Puerco, behind his desk with his back to the window. I squinted in the violent glare; my eyes began to tear. El Señor did not seem to notice my discomfort—or perhaps he was enjoying it?

"Sit down," he said.

I took a good look at the chair; it was a normal one, but I sat on it rather gingerly nonetheless. The glare from the window was now unbearable.

"Good morning," he began. "I hear you have done a very good job. Now I want to know if you are willing to talk." He paused and I waited, wondering. "You are crazy," he continued. "I can make you very rich if you have any sense at all."

"What is it that you have in mind?" I asked politely. El Puerco pulled out his big tufted-leather chair and sat down.

"I know you're successful at what you do," he said, as if I had not spoken. "But I also know what it costs to live in New York and I know all about American taxes. I do not believe it is possible for someone in decorating to make money."

"If you are talking about vast sums," I said, "you are perfectly right."

"I do not talk about anything else," he said. "Did you notice the furniture in this house? Every bit of it was made here in Havana, and it is of the finest quality money can buy. We have the best cabinetmakers, and wood carvers as a good as anywhere in the world. But there is one thing wrong: Cubans have no taste. Even this house is terrible. I know it." My eyebrows arched reflexively at that surprising admission. "People come here from South America to shop, and everything is so ugly that no one buys anything. We need a designer. If you will design for us, we'll make a killing."

"That is very tempting and flattering," I said, "but . . ."

"I do not flatter people," said my host. "I think of you as nothing more than an investment. I will put up all the money and give you a percentage of the business as well as a handsome salary upon which you will have to pay no American taxes. Who else would make you an offer like that?"

"But the trouble is," I said, "I'm not all that interested in furniture reproduction."

"You fool!" he exploded. "Do you think I would waste time on reproductions alone? I mean for you to design a whole line of contemporary furniture."

"But I really am only interested in pursuing my decorating career," I persisted.

"All right, then maybe part time."

"It's just so overwhelming," I said finally, "that I really had better think about this, if it's all right with you."

"All right," he said, gathering some papers impatiently; he knew what my answer was. "You have about three hours before your plane takes off. Good-by. Amuse yourself. And get the bill to me right away."

At the appointed hour, those two huge, black-coated Cubans appeared to take me off to the plane. When we arrived at the airport, one of them looked at me sternly. "There is a package aboard the airplane with you," he said. "You do not know what is in it." (It seemed I had heard all this before.) "When you arrive in New York . . ."

". . . I will ask the stewardess," I continued brazenly, "if it has been taken care of. Would someone kindly tell me what is in this package I'm risking my life for?"

"Risking your life, señor?" Both men laughed, their dark faces breaking into surprisingly affable grins. "It is only El Señor's silk shirts to be laundered in New York."

As for the bill, it was no great problem. Everything had been itemized before the goods were even shipped, and I had checked it all off against the shipping list as we uncrated it. A few days passed, and his stern-voiced secretary called to inform me that Sr. Puerco considered me a robber and a thief.

"What?" I asked.

"Do you realize, Mr. Baldwin," said the imperious woman, "what the duty is on all this merchandise?"

"Madame," I said, "I have no way of knowing what duty your country imposes."

"You will have the check tomorrow," she said, "minus the duty."

"Put El Puerco on the line," I commanded.

"You won't like what he has to say to you," she warned me.

"Never mind. Just put him on."

El Puerco came on. He told me everything in the house was junk and not worth my outrageous prices. (Perhaps he would rather have had his Cuban wood carvers decorate the place?) The check had already been mailed, he said, less the duty.

"That is the most dishonest, unbusinesslike thing I have ever heard of," I said. "I am not in the least involved in your country's duty."

"You should have found out," he accused.

"No, *you* should have," I retorted.

"Well," he said, "how do you think you are going to get the rest of the money?"

"Very simple," said I, in a quiet voice. "I shall tell everyone you know what you have done, especially our dear friend who got me involved with you in the first place."

That threat was enough to strike terror into the heart of even El Puerco. Our mutual friend is a woman capable of violent and righteous indignation—a woman, in short, to be reckoned with.

The bill was paid—in full.

CHAPTER 9

Mr. and Mrs. Gilbert Miller, 1945-1974

WHEN I RETURNED TO RUBY ROSS WOOD in July of 1945 after my tour of duty with the U.S. Army, my decorating career really began to take off. Mrs. Wood was good enough to insist upon publicity in my name, and word about my ability began to get around. Albert Kornfeld, editor of *House & Garden*, asked me to write a series of articles based on the *House & Garden* colors, to be illustrated with full-color drawings of rooms straight out of my imagination. Suddenly, I was no longer Ruby Ross Wood, Inc. I was *William Baldwin*, of Ruby Ross Wood, Inc.

Practically the first person to call me was Mrs. Gilbert Miller. The job was actually to be for her niece, Mrs. Warren Pershing, but we three all worked together wonderfully well, and with happy results. Anyone could tell right off that Kitty Miller was a woman of great taste and decorating experience. But over the years she has proved a kind and devoted friend as well. Together, and with her husband, Gilbert, we decorated their New York apartment, a room in their London house, and the whole of their house in Mallorca.

In matters of decorating, Kitty Miller knows exactly what she wants, and her choices are unfailingly correct. She insists upon practicality; everything has to work. The tea table, for instance, must be placed not only where it will look best, but where it will work best. The grog tray is always near the door so the butler can get to it without having to walk on everyone's feet. Kitty is a superb organizer when it comes to the workings of her households; one is never aware of the well-oiled mechanics that keep everything running so smoothly. She and her staff share an uncommon mutual loyalty.

One of the reasons I love to work with Kitty is that she is as extravagant as she is practical—probably the best combination of qualities. She abhors waste—which is, of course, the greatest sin in decorating—but she demands the most beautiful design and highest-quality workmanship. Although she will never spend money just to spend money, she is an extremely luxurious woman.

"The test of a truly elegant woman," Duarte Pinto-Coelho, Spain's leading decorator, once said to me, "is the contents of her handbag." Well, I have seen the insides of Kitty's handbags: everything in them, from lipstick to cigarette case to all those other mysterious things women carry, is chosen with care, and is invariably the most ravishing thing of its kind Kitty can find. Her good taste prevails in her dress and jewelry. She has always worn very simple clothes, beautifully cut and tailored, and, much to her credit, has always had a second sense about what not to wear—a trait some other women I have known would do well to develop.

The great French jeweler Jean Schlumberger told me after he had worked with

Kitty that he had never had a client more open to suggestion, yet with such sure instincts about jewelry. "She knows just how the weight of an earring affects the way it hangs," he said. "And how important it is to have her necklaces and bracelets of exactly the right scale." Indeed, she wears the most precious jewels with total unself-consciousness, as if she were wearing no jewelry at all.

Kitty's husband, Gilbert, whose father was England's great actor-manager Henry Miller, was enormous and bald, except for an immaculately trimmed fringe of hair. He had a deep gruff gravelly voice that whispered or growled or roared, according to his mood. I was not sure of Gilbert at first. He was blazingly intelligent, spoke many languages, and had a wonderful sense of humor. He hated misinformation of any kind and he loathed untruths. If the truth be told, he was an arrogant know-it-all, but the trouble was he practically did. Once, at dinner, Gilbert asked me a question and I answered him rather hesitantly. "Well," he shot back, "shut up if you don't know what you're talking about." Next day he discovered I had been right. He apologized at once to me, and never again did he speak to me like that. In fact, Gilbert became one of my staunchest supporters and a true friend.

Kitty and Gilbert had for each other the kind of love that is a pleasure even for outsiders to see. Gilbert was a brilliant raconteur, and Kitty, who must have heard all his stories on hundreds of occasions, always looked as fascinated as if she were hearing them for the first time. If in the middle of his story Gilbert forgot a pertinent piece of information, he would call down the table to his wife: "What ship were we on, Kitty?" or "What was the date of that, anyway?" And she, with the total attention she always gave everything and with her remarkable memory, would answer without a second's hesitation.

Opposite: *The banker Jules Bache left his dazzling collection of paintings, sculpture, and furniture to the Metropolitan Museum. His daughter, Mrs. Gilbert Miller, had the privilege of choosing her favorite picture, and it was to hang in her New York residence during the winter months that she and Mr. Miller occupied it. Mrs. Miller chose Goya's portrait of a child, popularly known as "The Red Boy." To celebrate the hanging of the great picture in their drawing room, the Millers sent cards for cocktails, to meet "Don Manuel Osorio de Zúñiga."*

Elsa Maxwell—whom Cole Porter called "Miss Liar" even to her face—couldn't place Don Manuel. She telephoned Margaret Case of VOGUE *and said, "Who's this Spaniard the Millers are introducing? I've never heard of him. Is he UN?"*

Miss Case of VOGUE *replied, "You'll know him when you see him. He always dresses in red, and he always has with him his two cats, a magpie, and a cage of finches."*

*Miss Margaret Case with
Woodson Taulbee and me*

*Programs for my two theatre
enterprises with Gilbert Miller*

Gilbert was as luxurious as his wife, and doted on fine clothes. Once, when I arrived at the Miller's London house after a night flight on which I had had very little sleep, Gilbert allowed me only a small nap and lunch before whisking me straight to his Savile Row tailor. By 5:00 P.M. we had chosen a complete wardrobe—for *me*—including some wonderful tails.

Gilbert was also intensely interested in his surroundings, and loved to be involved in decorating plans. I was glad to have him be, and why not? He demanded top quality in everything, and his trust in me was total. He thought me actually better than I really was, a wonderful compliment that also forced me to surpass myself. One summer day, Gilbert wrote me from England that he had "found in Paris the most beautiful yellow silk serge and matching border" and could I "have it made up into curtains for my room? And let's paint the room Versailles Grey." I had to spend an entire afternoon at the Metropolitan Museum of Art to discover what on earth "Versailles Grey" was.

Gilbert's trust in me wavered only once—on account of the dining room in New

94

York. The big square room was tenanted by a magnificent set of eighteenth-century Chippendale mahogany chairs Kitty had inherited from her father, the banker Jules Bache. For many years it was just a dull, conventional room, with a dark-brown rug, bony-white walls and silk curtains. The only thing that saved it was Kitty's exquisite china and linen and flowers—and some of the best food in New York.

While Kitty and I were having lunch one day, she suddenly stopped eating and looked darkly around the room.

"I don't intend to put up with this awful room another minute," she said. "I am going to send these chairs to be auctioned. I want banquettes, and nice copies of Louis XVI chairs that you can paint white."

"Well, Kitty," I said flatly, "I won't do it." The room would never take banquettes. And besides, it wasn't the chairs that were wrong for the room, it was the room that was wrong for the chairs. I persuaded her to try an experiment before doing anything rash.

I brought in a new rug, a black Bessarabian with wonderful reds and pinks. The ceiling and woodwork would remain the same bony-white, as would the curtains, which were perfect. The only change we would make was to glaze the walls the warm vivid color of strawberry sherbet. The room suddenly became appetizing, a pleasure to be in. And it set off all Kitty's lovely things. Kitty loved it.

But not everyone was pleased. Gilbert, in fact, was horrified. "What have you done?" he roared.

Although I told myself that this was just a fine example of masculine resistance to change and nothing more, I was a little worried that Gilbert would begin to question my over-all competence. It had always been so reassuring to have his unshakable support and trust.

A month later, at one of the Millers' celebrated lunch parties, I overheard Gilbert talking to a pretty young woman on his right. "Look what we did to this room," he said. "Don't you think this is a wonderful color?" As if he had painted it himself!

The ultimate proof of Gilbert's trust in me came one day when he telephoned from London. He had just bought the American rights to *The Reluctant Debutante*, a wildly successful play by William Douglas-Home, and he wanted me to design the sets.

What a thrill! I had never had any experience in scenic design, but that didn't faze Gilbert. Since I did not belong to a union, he told me I would be working with Raymond Sovey, who did—an extremely kind and talented man who had designed sets for many successful productions.

The set for *The Reluctant Debutante* was to be an Adam room in a flat in a beautiful house in Eaton Square, in the Belgravia district of London, that an attractive couple had rented for the purpose of launching their daughter in London society. To my amazement Gilbert insisted the set be built of solid wood; we could have installed it as paneling in a private house! Sovey told me I could expect to see Gilbert on stage checking out the set just before dress rehearsal. He would kick the doors, Sovey told me, to see if they trembled; he would open and close them from both sides to make sure no entrance or exit would be ruined by a door that stuck. There was nothing ever fake about Gilbert Miller.

I chose for the room a pale lilac trimmed with white—a very Adam combination and a good background for flowers and porcelains. Sovey made the color come true with theatrical lighting—a science in itself, I discovered. We used Adam and Regency chairs and tables painted black or white with gold, and a large comfortable sofa and chairs slip-covered in a ravishing chintz of jade green with a *chinoiserie* design that I bought from Rose Cummings for twenty-five dollars a yard—very expensive indeed in 1956. My own workroom did the slip covers and made the oyster-white taffeta curtains for the bow window. This was no paper-moon make-believe set!

At the first dress rehearsal, in New Haven, I had a terrible moment: on the beautiful white Adam mantel stood a pair of porcelain *cachepots* filled with flowers, and when the leading lady, Adrienne Allen, stood stage center for a big scene, I saw to my horror that she had three heads—her own and those two *cachepots*. It was theatre perspective that played the trick, Sovey explained, breaking into helpless laughter as I hastily substituted a pair of crystal candelabra.

The male lead, the brilliant English comedian Wilfrid Hyde-White, came to me trembling because the chintz was green. "Green," he said, wild-eyed, "is the symbol of inescapable bad luck." It was my first taste of theatre-folk superstitions, of which, I was to learn, there are hundreds, each more foreboding than the last.

There was also an uproar over a certain troublesome stool downstage. The stool I selected did not suit the male juvenile, who felt it was unbecoming to his long legs. So, on my next train trip from New York to New Haven, I lugged up another stool. This the leading lady refused to sit on because it was too high. I cheerfully produced a third choice, which Kitty immediately pronounced cheap and hideous.

"This stool is very conspicuous," she said. "You go and buy the prettiest real nineteenth-century Regency stool you can find, and to hell with the actors." It was the best advice on scenic design I ever received.

The debutante was delectably played by Anna Massey—the daughter of Adrienne Allen and Raymond Massey—who, having been a brilliant hit in the London production, was appearing on the American stage for the first time. The director was Cyril Ritchard, and Kitty Miller herself had selected the costumes. With that kind of talent, the play couldn't possibly miss.

We opened in New Haven to very favorable notices. I could hardly wait until October 10, 1956—the morning after the Broadway opening night. The play was a smashing success; all the reviews were accolades. But the comments on the sets gratified me most of all. "The mauve and white drawing room is in the very best Mayfair

The petit salon *in the Millers' New York apartment: an all-beige
room spark lit by three jewels: a Renoir above the mantel and one above the
Louis XVI desk, and, by the window, a Fantin-Latour*

manner," one critic enthused, and Brooks Atkinson, drama critic for the New York *Times*, wrote that the "fashionable London drawing room shines extravagantly."

Success served only to whet Gilbert's appetite. It wasn't long before he bought another play, *Patate*, a French comedy by Marcel Achard that had been running for years and years in Paris. (A *patate* is a sweet potato, but colloquially it means a "patsy" or "fall guy.")

Patate was a disaster from the first rehearsal. Irwin Shaw's translation was literal and wooden: the English had none of the flair and sparkle of the French. Then who should be cast as the *patate* but Tom Ewell, about the most homespun of American actors. It was whispered that Mr. Ewell was having not only himself psychoanalyzed, but the part as well. So far, this play did not have a particularly French flavor. Which was, I could see, at the very least unfortunate, because it was very Gallic indeed.

There were to be two sets for this play. One was the drawing room of a *nouveau riche* in Paris. It was deliberately overflowered and overdecorated. Raymond Sovey and I got permission from the Metropolitan Museum to copy the Louis XVI *boiserie* from the Hôtel de Tessé—a great eighteenth-century Paris house. It was reproduced so exactly that we could have switched with the museum with no one the wiser. The second-act set was a flat in Paris, much humbler, but done with much greater flair.

The play opened in New Haven. I sat with Gilbert and Achard, hearing what to me sounded like a lot of terribly stilted words being not very well delivered. I was surprised that Gilbert said nothing; he was such a perfectionist. Then I remembered what a great linguist he was and I knew that he was sitting in that New Haven theatre hearing the play in its witty French.

Our second pre-Broadway tryout was in Atlantic City in the dead of winter. The famous boardwalk was covered with snow, which kept on falling. I wondered if we'd have any house at all.

The theatre was so cold when the Millers and I arrived from New York that I had to keep my coat and gloves on when I went on stage to check things over. It was my responsibility to see that everything was in exactly the right spot. If an actor was supposed to take ten steps, then turn and pick up a letter from a table, that table had better be right there—or else quite a remarkable ad-libbed performance might take place. If anything did have to be moved, I could not simply pick it up and move it. Because I was not a member of the union, I was not allowed to touch a single thing. Instead, I had to "direct" a team of unionized workmen; the union rules said that every piece of furniture, no matter how small, had to be carried by two men. Picture two enormous muscle-bound men, one on each side of a Victorian chair a four-year-old could lift with one hand!

As I went about this ludicrous business on stage, the playwright's wife arrived.

Although Mme Achard hadn't the slightest idea who I was or what I had to do with the production, she told me in the most pompous way that the set looked exactly like a Park Avenue apartment. Furthermore, she was, she said, horrified to see on the Louis XVI chimneypiece of pair of imitation eighteenth-century porcelain birds. "Birds," she shrilled in her chlorine voice, "are absolutely fatal bad luck." She pronounced the second-act set a replica of *Tobacco Road*.

"Well, Madame," said I—I would be having no more of this—"Ah guess it's mah Southern blood comin' out." Gilbert and Kitty roared with laughter. And Madame was for the time being silenced.

We all knew what lay ahead, but Gilbert brought the play to New York anyway. "Let's be extravagant," said Kitty, cheerful to the end, "and have all fresh flowers for opening night." So we ordered dozens of bouquets. Downstage was a huge porcelain urn filled with armfuls of carnations. At the first intermission I was seized by the back of my collar. I turned to meet the fiery glare of Mme Achard, my favorite person in all of Atlantic City, who now pointed to the carnations with a quivering finger. "We have no chance now," she whispered feverishly. "*Les oeillets*—the evil eye."

We got the New York notices we deserved, and the play closed almost immediately. It was some small compensation to me that a few of the critics mentioned my sets favorably, in passing.

For several years, Gilbert and Kitty, who made a great team of host and hostess, gave historic New Year's Eve parties in their New York apartment. First, there would be a seated dinner for fifty at little tables set up in the dining room. About a hundred more guests would come in later for music and dancing in the drawing room. Just before midnight, the dining room would reopen, on an absolutely Lucullan buffet. It was like having, and going to, two parties in a single evening.

Kitty and I had marvelous times decorating for those parties. Usually we limited ourselves to some special treatment for the four large drawing-room windows. There would be festoons of flowers or fruit, or some other festive motif. Most memorable of all was the year we used great masses of plumes in apricot, orange, and white. The party looked like a Louis XIV fete. There were always fresh flowers, of course, and plenty of them; but nothing was ever placed where it could possibly interfere with the flow and comfort of the throng.

The guests at these extravaganzas were quite simply the brightest sparklers of New York society. Kitty loved having beautiful people around, so, besides the array of ambassadors, leading stars of the theatre, writers, politicians, and people from the arts, there were lots of young women invited just to look lovely. Once, perhaps overzealous in her insistence on perfection, Kitty blew up at a woman who appeared two years in a row in the same dress, and never invited her again. That woman will never again underestimate Kitty Miller's memory.

The New York dining room arranged for a party. Little gilt chairs surround one of a pair of
tables for eight, all done up in pink-and-red cotton (the good chairs are lined up against the far wall).
The rug is Bessarabian; the walls the strawberry-sherbet color Gilbert Miller loved.

More than once I saw Arthur Rubinstein at the buffet, concentrating with intensity on the royal spread of delicacies before him, not uttering a word to anyone until his plate was full. He knew a good buffet when he saw one.

But it was not only in New York that the Millers were surrounded by fascinating people. One time, we three flew from London to Paris for a few days just to see how Paris looked that spring, and the Sunday after our arrival we were asked to tea at Le Moulin, the country house of the Duke and Duchess of Windsor. We arrived to find a small house party going on. It was the anniversary of their famous marriage, and all the people there that day also had been guests at their wedding in Candé in 1936. "There's plenty of time before tea," said the Duchess, who looked brilliantly brittle and chic, to the Duke, who was better dressed than anyone I have ever seen in the country. "Why don't you take Billy Baldwin to the gardens for a walk, and don't forget that he came from Baltimore, too."

Those gardens were the Duke's greatest passion and delight in France. He had designed them all, working closely with the gardeners, always speaking in German. It was a memorable experience for me, an American, to be walking in a garden in France listening to a former king of England speak German. The gardens were vast, and filled with a variety of plants and flowers. As we turned a corner, the Duke stopped to admire a low green ground cover.

"Look at that beautiful ground cover," he said rather wistfully. "It was given me by an American friend, from her own garden, and I can't remember its name."

I am certainly no gardener, but I knew that that particular plant grows all over Maryland. "Could it be pachysandra?" I offered.

"Good for you!" said the Duke, genuinely delighted. "Of course that's what it is." When we returned to the house for tea, the Duke was still smiling. "You didn't tell me," he said to his Duchess, "that your Baltimore friend is a horticulturist."

A frequent visitor at the Millers' house in Mallorca, as well as at their houses in London and New York, was Miss Margaret Case, whom I had known from my earliest days in New York. Maggy was a brilliant editor on *Vogue*—the bride of *Vogue*, people used to say, because it was her bible and her life. No one has ever had a more delicious sense of humor. Until her death, on the very day she was expected at Kitty's in Mallorca, she was militantly loyal to the Millers; indeed, in many ways she was Kitty's best friend.

Once Gilbert was your friend, he was your friend for life. And that included your private life. At Drungewick Manor House, their country house in Sussex, he used to burst into my room at whatever hour he pleased to wake me in the morning, and sit there while I had my breakfast, passing comments on everything I ate. He was in his element when I asked him questions. It didn't matter what about—he knew something about everything. And how he loved to explain! Sometimes he explained things without even being asked.

One morning another guest persuaded me to get up early and have breakfast with him out on the terrace. We were sitting there, quietly enjoying the great peace and silence, when Gilbert suddenly came tearing out of the house, his dressing gown flapping, absolutely furious with me.

"I looked everywhere for you, even in the john," he raged. "I thought you were dead. If you're not going to be in bed in the morning, you might at least have the decency to tell me."

Another day, at lunch, Gilbert suggested that after his nap we might take a drive so he could show me the local houses and gardens. He promised we would be back at Drungewick in time for tea. I had no doubt of that, for Gilbert loved his tea and all the little cakes and sweets that went with it. He became a child at the sight of a petit four.

"Well, come along then, dear boy," growled Gilbert after his nap.

"You don't know what you're in for," warned Kitty. "To drive with Gilbert at the wheel is the most terrifying experience in life."

"Oh, Kitty." I laughed. "You exaggerate."

"Well, at least you can be glad he has given up his airplane." She sighed, remembering the not-so-far-off days when Gilbert used to fly his own plane from London to Drungewick on weekends and she invariably arrived in a state of nervous collapse.

The car was tiny and English, barely able to hold Gilbert. I was firmly wedged into one corner, praying the little latch would hold. The motor started, and off we went, racing along the lovely countryside.

Suddenly, I was pitched headlong into the dash. The car had slammed to a stop in front of a tree. I thought we had crashed. But Gilbert began enthusiastically to recite the name and history of the tree. I rubbed my forehead, trying to be appreciative. Without warning, he floored the accelerator, throwing me back into the seat, and the car lurched off to the next attraction. Thus did Gilbert conduct our entire tour. His conversation was nonstop and, once I got used to the transportation, very interesting. He knew every tree, every bush, every house, and every field, and, as he described them, he would look either out the side window, the better to appreciate their beauties, or at me, the better to make his point. Never at the road. Honking horns and squealing brakes accompanied us for most of our trip; motorists screeched to sudden stops behind us, or roared around us in exasperation.

"Now *that* looks like a beautiful house," I remarked. "Just barely visible above the trees across that meadow." Instantly, Gilbert swerved off the road, and we went tearing like a gunshot across the open field to get a better look.

Presently, the road ended in a lovely little village of simple early-Tudor cottages around a circular green.

"You are too young to know, dear boy," Gilbert said, gesturing with both hands

*The New York salon, a sunny straw-yellow room with
a contemporary linen rug and accents of shrimpy pink—a
delightful setting for Mrs. Miller's favorite little boy.*

Drungewick Manor House, the Millers' country house in England,
whose dining-room wing dates from the twelfth century.
The gardens, here celebrating the English springtime with
apple blossoms and narcissuses, were designed by Peter Coats.

off the wheel, "that that house was lived in by one of the most notorious actresses."
The car veered into the grass. "My father was a great *friend* of the lady's," said Gilbert,
raising one eyebrow and grinning lasciviously. He got the car back onto the pavement
and guided it around the green. "The house has one of the most beautiful rooms of
linenfold paneling in England," he continued. "I'll take you in to see it."

He jammed on the brakes and I was practically thrown out of the car. He got out
and walked the short distance to the door, while I unfolded myself and hurried along
to catch up with him.

The house, of course, was occupied. We could hear voices and laughter coming
from the garden, and what sounded like quite a heated tennis match. Gilbert opened
the front door as if it were attached to his own house, and strode right in.

Two ladies, perhaps guests, were talking to each other in the drawing room.
When they saw us, their eyes widened with alarm. Gilbert, unabashed, walked down
the hall to the room he wanted to show me. He only wanted to please *me*. It was a
remarkable room indeed, and I appreciated its intricate workmanship as best I could
under the circumstances. Gilbert calmly explained the room's history to me, pointing
out all its beauties, as I stood nervously shifting my weight from one foot to the other.
Finally, he finished and we left the way we had come. But one of the ladies had told
her hostess about us, for a small woman appeared rather hesitantly in the doorway
when we were well on our way down the path to our car.

"Darling," roared Gilbert, although it was quite clear the poor creature hadn't the
faintest idea who he was. "My father and I used to come to this house, and I had to
show that Elizabethan room to Baldwin here. He is the finest decorator in America."
As if that explained everything. "It's getting late," he said as he forced his great bulk
into the resisting space behind the wheel. "We might even miss tea." A wave of
apprehension such as I had never seen on him crossed his face. It wasn't, I knew, the
late hour that worried him, but the possibility that those sweet little cakes would all be
gone by the time we got there. I crammed myself into my little corner, and away we
flew to the cakes at breakneck speed.

In the lovely flowered drawing room at Drungewick sat Kitty, all alone, behind a
tea table gleaming with silver and china and several platters of lavishly frosted cakes.
She was in a terrible state, and her handkerchief was twisted beyond recognition.

"I thought you both had been killed," she said, giving each of us her hand in
obvious relief. "Thank God you are finally home."

Gilbert had not the foggiest notion what she could be talking about. And, at any
rate, this was no time to become emotional. Not with a tea table full of the most
delectable things to eat. Kitty and I exchanged sympathetic glances, and we all sat
down to tea.

CHAPTER 10

Two Walks:
Jackie Kennedy, 1963;
Jackie Onassis, 1968

JACQUELINE BOUVIER KENNEDY knew I was going to be spending the weekend of November 16, 1963, with her friend Mrs. Paul Mellon in Upperville, Virginia, and asked if I could stop off and see her in Middleburg on my way down. Could I ever!

I was on the shuttle at the crack of dawn. At the airport, I was met by a starchy naval officer in an official State Department car. It was a warm and glorious Saturday, and the landscape flashed by in all its rich autumn colors as the car sped along the Virginia highways. Before long we came to a pair of great stone gateposts linked by a thick tarnished chain. A snappy-looking guard stepped smartly out of what looked like a sentry box, and flipped through my identification papers. When he was satisfied that we were perfectly harmless, he somewhat grudgingly unhooked the chain. The big lugubrious black car rumbled through. The driveway wound through the trees and led at last to a rather banal little house in the woods. The Kennedy Estate.

I was admitted by a prim Filipino who was more or less in charge of things, and led into a big living room whose walls were painted a strikingly unpleasant lox pink.

"Mrs. Kennedy is aware that you have had an early flight and a very early breakfast," recited the smiling little man. "She has instructed me to bring you breakfast in this room, after which she will see you." I was grateful for this considerate treatment. So often, after I have arrived somewhere, even by way of the most awkward travel arrangements, I am immediately taken to a room, my coat still on my back, and expected to "create."

While I was having my delicious (and enormous) breakfast, I looked around the room. Mrs. Kennedy had apparently been too occupied with affairs of state to give this place much attention. Not that it was bad; it was just totally unremarkable, without a bit of the famous Jackie flair. There were chintz curtains and slip covers that looked as if they were makeovers from somewhere else, one or two good-looking pieces of lacquer, the President's ubiquitous rocking chair—and that was it.

I stuffed myself to the point where I could not rationalize another bite and called for the houseboy to take my tray away. Presently, the room was filled with the radiance of the First Lady herself. She was dressed in beige jodhpurs and a black turtleneck sweater, with that marvelous thick dark hair of hers tumbling around her shoulders—and that smile!

"You are an angel to come here to this terrible house," she purred, crossing the room to perch beside me. "My husband doesn't like it here at all, but he knows the children and I love to come here to ride, and he knows he can rest here, so he puts up with it. But, you see, we really don't want to spend any money on it at all. Do you think you can pull it together?"

"I don't think the house is all that terrible," I said. "In fact, with a few changes and additions it can be made very pretty indeed. But it is going to be difficult to do anything as long as there is this paint on the walls."

"Thank heaven you're honest," she said.

The remedy was simple—we would just put on one coat of a much paler shade of the same color, which would make it look like a lovely soft apricot, instead of canned fish.

"Also," I said, warming to the project, "those two off-white slip covers will have to go."

The First Lady's face melted into a broad grin. "Thank you so much," she said. "I broke my neck to have those made and put on before you got here."

We toured the house. It was small, but adequate, and completely unpretentious. The children's rooms were to be left alone; in fact, nothing much was to be done anywhere else except in her own bedroom and a small empty room that she wanted to turn into a Moroccan-looking family room. The bedroom was quite sunny and dominated by a charming pink-and-white chintz. It needed really very little. I suggested a new chair and ottoman and some better reading lights. Mrs. Kennedy wanted to be sure that there would be some translucent cotton curtains she could draw by day, thus admitting the sun and simultaneously protecting her from peepers, a problem despite the heavy security.

The empty room was to have low banquettes and a low table for dining (she had recently returned from Morocco, where she had been positively seduced by the sumptuous low seating). This was where the television would be also, and everything had to be comfortable and relaxed and warm.

Mrs. Kennedy breathed a long sigh. "I suppose we'll have to have a rocking chair in here, too. You were so polite not to mention the one in the living room."

"It is not a question of manners," I assured her. "I think the rocking chair is perfectly fine. And I can think of nothing more presumptuous or less professional than for a decorator to suggest the removal of the favorite chair of the President of the United States."

"Speaking of the President," Mrs. Kennedy said, "I am going to be terribly rude and tell you that he must not catch you here. He is at the moment in mid-air on his way back from making an important speech. He's very tired, and since he doesn't much like to come here anyway, I must be certain his privacy is absolute—and no decorator!" Again that smile.

"But before you go"—and I felt the light touch of her fingers on my sleeve—"I'd like you to see my husband's room and bath. I'll just take you to the threshold and you can tell me if you see any evidence whatsoever that anyone has ever set foot inside those rooms."

I followed her to a very attractive beige room with eighteenth-century red-and-white *toile de Jouy*. Except for a dressing gown and fresh pajamas laid out on the bed, the room looked totally uninhabited: no Kleenex or half-read books on the bedside tables, no cuff links strewn on the chest, no newspapers piled beside the chair. Nothing. It was as austere as a museum; I half expected to see a little sign that said, "President Lincoln slept here." I walked on through to the bathroom. To judge by the appearance of it, I might have been the first human being ever to enter.

"I don't understand it," Mrs. Kennedy said. "I leave wonderful soaps and shaving lotions and things for him in here—and they simply disappear into the drawer. He's just not interested." She shrugged, then tilted her pretty head. "And now, Mr. Baldwin, I'm afraid you, too, must disappear."

She saw me to the door, where the big black car was waiting.

"I'm going to Dallas with the President next week," she said, "so there's no need to hurry with your ideas—and estimates. We'll have another happy meeting when I get back. . . ."

About three weeks after Dallas, Mrs. Kennedy called me herself from Washington to ask if I could come to see her.

"I know it is inconsiderate of me to ask," she said in a voice whose sadness could not be concealed, "but could you come very soon?"

"Any time," I said.

"Tomorrow?"

Once more I was up with the birds to catch the earliest shuttle to Washington. The plane took off in a fearful blizzard—and was the last to land before the airport was shut down. I was met by the secret service and whisked to the house of Governor and Mrs. Averell Harriman, where Mrs. Kennedy and her children had been living since the Johnsons had moved into the White House. The Governor and his wife, Marie, had generously given the former First Lady their own house and moved to the Georgetown Inn. Mrs. Kennedy was eager to cut the Harrimans' inconvenience short —and also to get Caroline and John into bedrooms of their own and a state of normalcy once again, insofar as that could be managed.

Throngs had gathered, shivering in the snow, before the house. The police had cleared a space directly in front, and into this clearing the secret service steered our car. When I got out, I heard not a sound from the multitudes. They stood silent and sad-faced; a few were gaping, others grieving. Somehow, it made me think of Russia.

A secret-service man rang the doorbell, and Mrs. Kennedy, dressed very simply in black wool, came to the door to greet me. This time, that smile was sad.

"It was so kind of you to come in this terrible weather," she said. "I'm trying to get away with the children over the Christmas holidays, and before we leave I want to take you across the street to show you the house I've just bought. I want to get the children into it as soon as I can."

She took my coat and led me to a little sitting room, where I was introduced to her sister, Mrs. Lee Radziwill, and three men who had been constant companions and aides of the late President. The men were all as Irish as Jack Kennedy himself, and Mrs. Kennedy had affectionately dubbed them the "Murphia." I took the Bloody Mary and sandwich someone offered and sat down to listen to them reminisce about that last evening in the Dallas hotel. . . .

(That night the Murphia had been in the sitting room of the President's hotel suite trembling because they had forgotten to pack evening shoes for the black-tie dinner the President was to attend. They had therefore laid out, with his dinner jacket, a pair of very nice brown shoes. The President meanwhile was whistling gaily in the shower. Then the shower stopped, and the men waited. A loud oath resounded from the bedroom. Followed by an awful silence. "Oh well," came the President's reasonable voice, addressing himself, "if it's color TV, we'll just start a new style.")

Mrs. Radziwill went to the window. "The snow has just about stopped," she said.

"Yes," Mrs. Kennedy said. "We really should be going." So the two sisters and a secret-service man and I bundled up again. And Jackie and I went for our first walk together.

The police had cleared a path for us through the people who were lined up as far as the eye could see on both sides of the street. As we walked down the block, they just stood watching, almost reverently.

The house was a handsome Georgian structure raised high off the street by several flights of steps. Mrs. Kennedy had some photographs of the children's White House rooms; their rooms in this house were to be exactly the same. I had brought with me some samples of rugs and wallpaper, and we picked out a few of these and planned the paint and curtains and general furniture layout. We worked methodically, but without much enthusiasm. I must confess that I have never attempted anything so difficult. Of course, I knew I could decorate the house, but I felt so terribly superfluous. I looked at my client—she was only thirty-four. Losing someone one loves is a very private matter, and here she was, forced to share her grief with the whole world. Her life had been absolutely shattered, her family uprooted, and I was faced with trying to make her feel at home somewhere. It seemed almost hopeless. I promised to come any time she wanted me, and to supervise the work myself. I could do that much.

Everyone worked double time to get the house ready for the little family to move in. Naturally, there remained much to be done, and I was often in Washington seeing

to the paint and curtains, and making final decisions about the layout. Every time I went, it seemed there were more spectators outside. Not only were they lining the sidewalks, but there was bumper-to-bumper traffic now as well. The new Kennedy home had become one of the tourist sights of Washington.

"It's very upsetting," Mrs. Kennedy told me later. "Women are always breaking through the police lines trying to grab and hug and kiss the children as they go in and out."

I could see for myself how people were peering into the enormous windows—I was shocked at how easy it was to see into the house, despite its great elevation. Once, I arrived in late evening, and the lights inside the house were making a doubly interesting show for the spectators. It got so I made it a habit to draw the curtains the minute I got there.

On one of my visits, I arrived to find Mrs. Kennedy busy putting the books away in the living-room bookcases. Grouped on the floor against the walls of the big white room were her very personal and utterly beautiful collection of drawings of all schools, many of animals, ready for us to hang. This collection was the clue to her rare taste— intellectually and aesthetically. I knew what the books and those drawings would do with the apricot silk curtains she had ordered. In the middle of the room, opposite the fireplace, there was an oversized and overstuffed sofa in yellow velvet; in back of it was a Chinese lacquer altar table.

I had never seen anyone looking so bereft.

"Look," she said, opening some boxes. "I have some beautiful things to show you." She produced, one after another, small pieces of Greek sculpture and Roman fragments, each one a rare treasure. "These are the beginnings of a collection Jack started," she said in a very quiet voice. She began putting the lovely things all around the room. "It's so sad to be doing this. Like a young married couple fixing up their first house together. I could never make the White House personal—so many rooms around me that I knew were empty. . . ." Her voice was filled with profound desolation. "Oh, Mr. Baldwin," she said, "I'm afraid I'm going to embarrass you. I just can't hold it in any longer." And, sinking to a chair, she buried her face in her hands and wept. I felt so awkward, wanting to comfort her, not knowing how. I sat quietly nearby.

Finally, she looked up, dabbing at her eyes with a handkerchief.

"I know from my very brief acquaintance with you that you are a sympathetic man," she said, barely audibly. "Do you mind if I tell you something? I know my husband was devoted to me. I know he was proud of me. It took a very long time for us to work everything out, but we did, and we were about to have a real life together. I was going to campaign with him. I know I held a very special place for him—a unique place. . . ."

She talked on and on, very quietly, very sadly, about her life with Jack Kennedy, and the room filled with her terrible loneliness.

"Can anyone understand how it is to have lived in the White House, and then, suddenly, to be living alone as the President's widow? There's something so final and passé about it. And the children. The world is pouring terrible adoration at the feet of my children and I fear for them, for this awful exposure. How can I bring them up normally? We would never even have named John after his father if we had known . . ." I think of that as the moment Jackie Kennedy began to be the extraordinary mother she has become.

"Let's have a little lunch," she said, pulling herself together with great effort. "This is terrible; I have made you miss shuttle after shuttle. Please, Billy, you must call me Jackie now."

We did get some things done after lunch—at least we talked about her bedroom, which was the big stickler. And I left for New York with a long list of things to do. But I still felt woefully inadequate. I should have made a lovely gay bedroom for her; she needed so badly to have something lovely and gay. But it was hard. The atmosphere was so sad. I gave my entire professional attention to that house; yet I felt thwarted, even diminished, by it.

Early one morning, my office telephone rang. It was Jackie.

"I must entrust you with a secret," she said. "It's the kind of thing somebody can make a lot of money on, but I must be honest with you."

"Well, what is it, Jackie?" I asked, although I already had a feeling . . .

"Please cancel any work you haven't actually yet begun. Naturally, I'll pay for what's already been started. But I just cannot live here in this house in Washington. I'm moving to New York."

One day at the end of October 1968, my secretary, Miss Schwick, came running breathlessly into my office. "There's an overseas call for you, Mr. Baldwin," she said. "Maybe it's your client in Mallorca. It's impossible to understand. Could you take the call?"

"Of course," I said; then, into the receiver, "Hello!" There was some static, followed by a faint, impatient masculine voice, heavily accented.

"The *Christina* is calling Mr. Baldwin."

"This is Mr. Baldwin," I said.

"One moment. Madame Onassis." More static and a series of clicks, and then a very little voice:

"Billy, I need you. I need a friend. How soon can you come to see me?"

"Oh, Jackie, how good to hear from you," I said. My God, it was three days after their wedding. "But what do you mean by 'how soon'?"

"Tomorrow?"

Well, I couldn't make it that quickly, but I agreed to come the day after, with some photographs of furniture for her. Just a friendly little business trip.

"How long do you think I should plan to be with you?" I asked.

"Probably three days and two nights on Scorpios, possibly another night in Athens on your way back," she said. "Now don't you do anything. Ari and his secretary and Olympic will take care of everything."

So off I went to Greece, where I had never been. When I got off the plane, very tired indeed, I didn't see anyone at the gate to meet me, not a soul. I hadn't the slightest idea where to go. I found myself an information desk, behind which stood a beautiful Greek girl. I felt better already.

"I am Mr. Baldwin," I said, keeping things simple, "and I am the guest of Mr. Onassis, the president of this airline."

"Just a moment, sir," she said, her eyes widening as she picked up the telephone. There was a great deal of lively conversation in Greek and presently the girl turned to me, smiling. "Everyone knows you are expected, sir," she said, "and no one has any idea why you were not met. Mr. Onassis is very angry. The best thing for you to do now is take bus Number Seven to the Athens square where the Olympic office is. Mr. Onassis will be waiting there for you."

There was a terrible lot of excitement at the office building, a kinetic feeling of something really big going on. The unheralded arrival of a decorator from New York couldn't create *this* kind of stir. I was taken up to Onassis's floor. At the end of a long modern corridor, in an open doorway, stood a stocky figure, legs splayed, hands on hips. He was furious that I had not been met, but there were reasons. The whole building was rocking with the news that that very morning Onassis had consummated the acquisition of three huge Irish tankers. This enormous transaction put even the glory of his three-day-old marriage somewhat in the shadows; in fact, the press had taken pleasure in reporting that three times in the first couple of days of his honeymoon Onassis had left Scorpios for Athens. (This, of course, meant he was not happy with his bride. . . .)

"We'll lunch at my house, then go to Scorpios," he said. "So go to your hotel, shave, bathe, sleep well, and we'll call you when it's time."

No one had to suggest sleep a second time. I did exactly as I was told.

When I was called down after my delightful nap, I found the hotel lobby seething with people. Reporters swarmed all around, trying to get interviews with Onassis. I pushed through the crowd to his car, which, the second *he* came out and got in beside me, was besieged by television camera crews and reporters. They scrambled for their cars, and we were followed all the way through Athens to his house in the suburbs.

It was a lovely drive. The weather was fine, and Onassis took care to point out all the sights a tourist was likely to be interested in. The Acropolis. A few temples. I instantly felt that I had always known him.

The house reminded me of a Palm Beach house. No property to speak of, but lots of palm trees and hibiscus just the same. We stepped up to the terrace and through French doors to the living room, where the new Mrs. Onassis stood, dressed in a smart gray flannel dress. She smiled adorably at me and gave me a greeting that amounted to a sigh of relief. I was glad to see her so happy at last.

Ari's two famous sisters were at her side. One greeted me in English; the other just smiled and said, "No English." I was surprised to discover that Jackie, despite her brilliance at languages, still knew not a word of Greek. Everyone proceeded to laugh and chatter happily, except for the "No English" sister, of course, who just sat there smiling the whole time.

The room was full of shining new reproduction Napoleonic furniture in mahogany and gilt. It was very grand indeed, and looked as if Napoleon himself had bought it that morning.

"Billy," said Jackie, "you are about to have your first experience with a Greek lunch. I will kill you if you pretend to like it." I looked around, expecting to see three offended Greeks. Smiles. "Some of it is interesting and very good, but you must be very careful, and *very* honest." I promised on my honor. The trays were brought, and when they were emptied, other trays were brought, and so on through a multicourse lunch of remarkable hors d'oeuvres. Most of it was delicious. Some of it—well, I had been warned.

"This boy's all right," said Ari, wiping his mouth aggressively with his napkin. "We'll give him a treat. We'll go to Scorpios by helicopter. I'll meet you at the airport." And saying his affable good-bys all around, he was gone. A little while later, Jackie said, "I think it's time for us to go, too."

I walked with Jackie then, for the second time, out to the street, where the car was waiting amid an enormous cheering throng. My mind reeled back to our first walk in Washington that terrible winter, where the crowds stood silent in the snow. Here, everything was happiness and sunshine, and the masses of people were in love with Jackie, not mourning with her. We hustled into the car and drove off, followed by a triumphal horn-blowing cavalcade.

At the airport the crowd seemed to thicken and grow even more boisterous. Besides the citizens, there was a bedlam of professional Jackie-watchers and photographers, and frankly I was beginning to fear for her safety. It was only with the aid of Greek policemen that we were able to get into the helicopter at all. Ari, in the front seat with the two pilots, just turned to us and smiled; he was used to this kind of fun. I, on the other hand, had never seen the like of it. Reporters were crowding furiously in on us, rocking the helicopter from side to side. I think they were even on the roof.

"Jackie," I said, "I'm really afraid for your life. What can I do?"

"You just sit there and smile," she said, enjoying my unrest. "I'm sure we're being televised, and I'm sure it will be aired in the States, so just *sit still*." She grinned an exceedingly sly grin. "Maybe Sister Parish will see you."

Finally, there was a great roar, the crowd dropped away, and we were air-borne. The setting sun had turned the Ionian Sea into sparkling lapis lazuli. Back and forth we tacked, over beautiful Greece. We flew very low, and at several points we dipped disturbingly—I, at least, was disturbed—close to the hilltops. Ari explained over his shoulder the glories of Greece: there, he said, pointing down, is a monastery; and there is Corinth; and there the Straits of Corinth. Ari indicated a little island. "That's the one I almost bought," he shouted above the engine's whine, "before I got Scorpios."

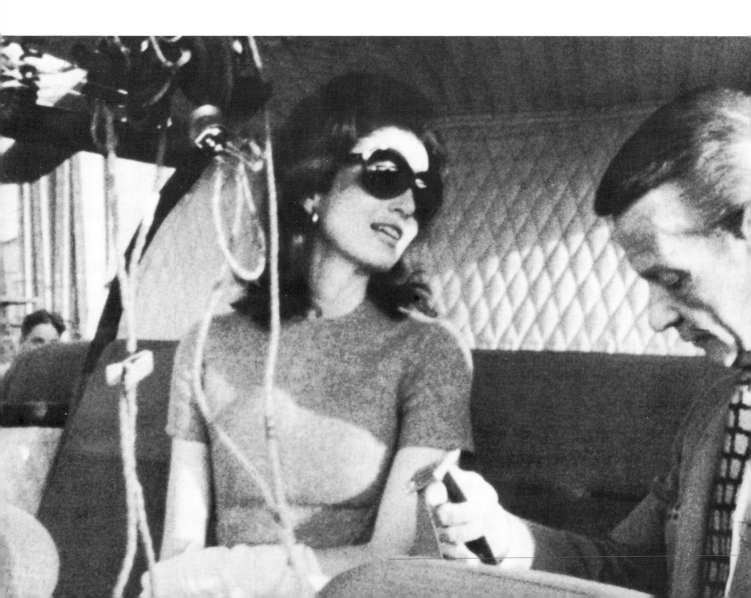

The landscape changed suddenly; in the deepening twilight I could see we were flying over tiers of long mountains, with little villages nestled in their valleys. As darkness fell, the village lights twinkled on, and then we passed another mountain and it was all dark again; then another twinkling village materialized, and so on, a repeating pattern of light and dark, until I began to think that Greece could really do with fewer mountains.

"Isn't Scorpios just beyond this one?" Jackie would say every time we approached another mountain. But it never was. Shifting in her seat, she leaned toward me confidentially. "I wish he had bought that first island," she said in a low voice.

At last there was below us a great black body of water, shining like polished onyx in the moonlight. It looked like a colossal lake, but Ari said it was an inlet of the sea. And there was Scorpios, a black matte patch on the slick surface of the water, with a brilliant welcome lantern: a great ship, all ablaze, anchored at the dock. The *Christina*. At some distance, in a fan formation around her, shone the lights of little boats.

"Who's that?" I asked Jackie.

"That," she replied, "is the press."

We landed on the helipad near the harbor. A carpet was laid on the ground, and standing at attention were the gray-haired captain of the *Christina* and the chief engineer, who flashed me a smile of solid-gold teeth.

Along the path to the ship I couldn't help noticing the appalling planting, like that in a neighborhood park, with scraggly little flowers sticking up. A pungent smell wafted in from the island—the smell of lavender.

The ship was four decks high and immaculately white, with a crew of sailors fresh from the laundry. Inside, it was the ugliest thing I had ever set eyes on. The epitome of vulgarity and bad taste. Entirely covered with thick wall-to-wall carpeting with tacky canvas runners. My very own stateroom, to which I was immediately taken, was about twenty feet long, low-ceilinged, and all done in Louis XV reproductions. It was embarrassingly elaborate, with pink taffeta everywhere, and plenty of gold. The bathroom was solid pink marble. But I must admit that, for all its vulgarity, the room was fantastically comfortable.

Before dinner, for which I had been instructed to dress casually, I was summoned to the saloon. The first thing that caught my eye was a coffee table, at least four feet square, piled high with Greek hors d'oeuvres, some of which I had met with before. Among the unfamiliars were pink fish eggs rarer than caviar. To wash all this down: a great flow of vodka. Ari and I sat for a few moments waiting for his bride. He was overwhelmingly charming. Several women I knew had told me he was the most charming man they had ever met. Presently, Madame

Onassis appeared in a scarlet sweater and a long white skirt. Through her luxuriant hair I could glimpse the famous diamond-and-ruby earrings Ari had given her as a wedding present and which *Life* had found so newsworthy.

The dining-room walls were covered with murals of naked little girls depicting the four seasons. They had been done by Vertez, a fashionable muralist of the thirties, and they were positively horrendous. Dinner was elaborate and very good, but the table was hideous, set with bad china and fancy glasses and silver, and the flowers were overdone. The saloon where we went for coffee had pale-apple-green French-paneled walls, and, again, French reproduction furniture built by the talented Greek cabinetmaker who had produced all that spit-polished Napoleonic furniture for the Athens house.

I had seen a pink marble bathroom, two elaborate saloons, and a dining room with naked little girls all over it—and that was enough for one day. My paltry night's sleep, all that vodka and rich food, the excitement of being in the royal party . . .

"I'm terribly sorry," I said, I hope not too groggily, "but I really do think I must say good night."

"Oh," said Jackie in a voice of genuine disappointment. "Soon we're going to be having some nice little treats, and you'll miss them."

Ari understood. "You've got to work like crazy in the morning," he said amiably, "so go to sleep. I'll see you for dinner tomorrow night; I fly to Athens at daybreak."

When I opened my eyes in the morning, the first thing I saw on a chair beside the door was a little bag made of some soft material and tied with a bunch of yellow flowers. I got right up and went over to have a look. The bag was filled with delicious-looking little cakes and candies and Turkish delight: the treats I missed. And a note from Jackie:

Billy: You missed your midnight sweets—and the houris have been kneading unguents all day long . . . After the zenith of the moon and our evening prayer, which is sweetened by Turkish delights, we have a dainty feast, and since, O Cruel Allah, you could not share it, before we find *La Belle aux Bois Dormant*, we drop these sweetmeats by your couch, to make voluptuous the dawn for you.

Mme Suleiman Le Brilliant.

All the friendliness and holiday atmosphere aside, I had not brought my photographs and notebooks to the *Christina* for nothing. Jackie was expecting her children for Christmas, and there was not a single bed on the island. There was, I was told, a small, corridorlike building containing a series of bedrooms and baths—all unfurnished, of course. To make a house of it, work had begun on the foundation for a large living-dining room and kitchen. Jackie did not want her family staying aboard the *Christina*, and I must admit I sympathized with her. My job was to work out the interior architecture and furnish the thing—all by Christmas, which by *my* calendar was less than two months away.

The gilt-toothed engineer and his kindly captain whisked me in a little car to the building spot. The men proudly pointed out their miles of superb concrete roadway, which, they did not realize, entirely spoiled the island's natural loveliness. Everywhere women dressed in heavy clothing the somber colors of a Braque painting—dark brown, gray, eggplant, and olive—bustled along, sweeping the white road as though it were carpet by the yard.

When we got away from the harbor and heliport area, the island became lush and beautiful, full of lovely groves and woods of marvelous trees that Onassis had brought there—as ballast on the *Christina*—from all over the world. The orange groves were superb. It was all a great surprise to me: I had expected Scorpios to be barren and naked white, stark and rocky, like pictures I had seen of other Greek islands. It was as verdant as Tuscany, but the smell of lavender, so welcome at first, was becoming heavy and oppressive, like the bow stroke of a string bass underscoring everything.

We came to a long pink building with a cloister: the bedroom wing. At the end of the cloister was the square excavation, swarming with workmen. There could not have been more laborers at work on the building of the pyramids. I was suddenly struck full force by the immensity of the project. The building was still largely on paper, the interior architecture had not been decided on yet (the two Greek cabinetmakers who had built all of Ari's furniture were coming the next day to discuss it with me), and I hadn't even begun to think about the decoration. I looked blankly down into the raw hole that I was expected to transform into livable quarters within six weeks.

The big surprise was that I seemed to be the only one with any misgivings. The workmen were all certain that everything would be finished precisely on schedule. "It will be," they assured me, "because it must be."

The building site was the most cheerful I had ever visited. The workmen were smiling and excited, humming away like bees. As we talked, I became aware of another hum—the sound of a distant engine growing louder and louder and closer and closer, until suddenly it was a frightening roar behind me. I spun around and saw a motorcycle driven by a sailor, with a passenger clad in a hot-rodder T shirt and faded-blue pants. It was Jackie! She was radiant, and absolutely delighted with herself. For the first time since I had seen her in Virginia, Jackie was really free.

She dismounted and walked through the property with me. The big room was to be rather masculine, we decided, and have not much color—mostly contemporary furniture and lineny fabrics in brown and black and white. In one corner there would be a banquette, and in front of a vast window a dining table and chairs—for once, a "picture window" was justifiable. The view was staggering, yet somehow sympathetic: from here the Greek mountains seemed very friendly! "I've just got to get Ari on land." She laughed. The bedrooms were to be printed cottons, all very fresh and clear, with one good piece of old furniture in each room.

The sailor rode the bike back to the *Christina*, and Jackie came with the captain and me in the car. We chose a circuitous route that wound to the very top of the island. From the vantage point of a peculiar clearing in the lush growth, we had an incredibly beautiful view down the hillside to the sea.

"This is where Ari plans to build his villa," Jackie said coolly. "I think he has in mind something like the Trianon at Versailles, or some kind of domesticated Acropolis. As far as I am concerned, there will never be a house here."

After lunch aboard the *Christina*, and after I had just spread all the plans out on the floor and started doing the furniture arrangement, Jackie announced she was going to have a swim.

"How about you?" she asked.

"Not me," I said, pencil in my teeth. "I've got lots to do."

She stepped on to a diving platform built like a pirate's walking plank, gave a little spring, and plunged headlong into the sea. I jumped up to watch. Jackie started swimming away from the ship. She swam for a long time, never breaking her stroke, and soon I had to shield my eyes and squint to see her clearly—a tiny black ripple in the water. I was glad of the sailors on duty watching her, but I worried nonetheless, and for all the work I got done while she was out there, I might as well have gone in swimming with her.

Finally, she was back, glistening, her soaking hair slicked back like some beautiful seal. She dried off, slid into a white terrycloth robe, and sat down to rest beside me in the late-afternoon sun.

Sometime just after dark we heard the sound of an airplane engine. Jackie sprang to her feet and rushed to station herself at the diving platform. She stood very still, searching the sky. Suddenly, she was bathed in light from some sort of spotlight on the plane, and she responded with a joyous wave of her hand. When her heavenly light was switched off, Jackie came back inside and stood before me utterly frozen. I dared not speak. Eventually, she relaxed.

"I heard the splash of the landing," she murmured. "Thank God he's safe."

Never again will I witness a performance of *Tristan and Isolde* without thinking of that moment. That night on the *Christina* my ears were ringing with Wagner's divine music.

We were all together again at dinner—a splendid time, I thought, to discuss the plans for the house. But although Ari was enthusiastic, he made it clear that he did not want to be involved in the details.

"Billy," he said, "I will help you all I can with getting the house completed, but you have to get one thing straight. This house I want to be a total surprise. I trust you, and Jackie and I don't want to know anything about it. I have only one request. Can there be a long sofa by the fire so I can lie and read and nap and watch the flames?"

Some time later, a spurious rumor was started in a column in a Washington paper and circulated worldwide that Onassis and I had discussed plans for the house while Jackie stood behind him shaking her head yes or no at everything he said. That paper should be ashamed of itself.

Before bed aboard the *Christina*, Ari took me to his study. I was shocked: it was one of the greatest rooms I had ever been in, on land or sea. It was very personal, very masculine, and full of books, and there was a wonderful El Greco. It almost made up for the horror of the rest of the ship.

Next morning the Greek cabinetmakers arrived bright and early, and we got down to work. Mercifully, Ari had given me permission to make whatever changes I wanted in their proposals. I began slashing right and left. Out went all those tricky elaborations of detail. Out went all that fussiness. My objective was to simplify, simplify, simplify. Of course, the two Greeks didn't much like what I was doing, but I gave as my excuse the shortness of the time, and they really had to admit that yes, simpler was faster. They were blindly confident as ever that it would all be finished by Christmas. Trying to muster my own confidence, I found that I had my fingers crossed.

I said good-by to the Onassises on the topmost deck of the *Christina*. The great ship was dazzling in its immaculate whiteness, as, indeed, was its new mistress in white sailor pants and a black pull-over. We drank champagne in sparkling crystal glasses against a blue sky equally as sparkling.

It seemed to me that this woman was basking in a reward for her performance on that long-ago day, which earned for her and her country the admiration and sympathy of the world. How far she had come to this new happiness.

As for my Greek host, he excelled in hospitality more than anyone I have ever known—and I do come from the South.

When I got back to New York, I mobilized my entire crew. There was not a moment to lose. The minute each piece of furniture, or curtain, or slip cover was acquired or made, it went to its berth on the nightly Olympic jet to Athens that Ari had put at my disposal. We worked at breakneck speed, and somehow, by the grace of a not-so-cruel Allah, we got it done in time.

I never saw the finished house. The only evidence I have that Jackie was able to persuade her husband to go ashore was the cable I received just after Christmas. "Happy New Year," it said, "and congratulations on the Erechtheum of Billy, which we are now enjoying. Love, Ari, Jackie."

CHAPTER 11

Metamorphosis, 1946-1973

WHEN YOU WANT TO TRANSFORM A ROOM into an entirely different animal, change the color. To illustrate this law of decorating nature, here are two apartments, both of them my own, that over the years I character-changed radically— just by switching colors. The first apartment was in Amster Yard, the little oasis on Forty-ninth Street between Second and Third avenues, where I lived in the forties and fifties. The second is my present apartment in the East Sixties. As time passed, I would sometimes replace a chair or table with something better, or do a bit of simple rearranging, or perhaps acquire a new picture. But it is color that, in rooms as in caterpillars, makes the transformation startling.

1946, Amster Yard: The whole apartment—living room, bedroom, and hallway—is painted dark shiny green, a revival of Elsie de Wolfe's famous green rooms. To let the painter know exactly what I had in mind, I had the audacity to give him as a sample a gardenia leaf that I had licked to a glisten. The curtains are emerald-green silk, the furniture slip-covered with a darker green textured silk. I loved this color scheme so much I vowed never to change it.

1951: I changed it entirely. Now the whole apartment is painted white. The furniture is vivid-yellow satin, the curtains yellow silk (this was the first time Thaibok silk, imported as dress material, was ever used in decoration). On the bedroom wall hangs a beautiful brush-and-ink by Matisse. Above the living-room sofa hangs a dark Spanish still life of wonderful apples, their color icy red, like a star. When Pauline de Rothschild saw it, she exclaimed, "I have never before seen red used as a cold color!"

1955: Four years later and the place is barely recognizable. Practically everything— walls, sofa, curtains—is covered with a white-on-white French linen-and-rayon brocade so extraordinary I couldn't resist buying it by the mile. With this lovely stuff, I used much better furniture and much subtler color: apricot cut velvet on the chairs by the fire; brown-and-cream cut velvet on a very fine French chair near the sofa; and for a table covered to the floor, yards of brown satin. Above the sofa hangs an English painting of hounds, which lived with me for years in Amster Yard and then for a bit in my present apartment before moving to San Juan. Note that the furniture arrangement has never changed.

1963, Midtown: A night room, since night was the only time I was ever in it. Walls are painted Coromandel black-brown, my all-time favorite, with a Korean

Amster Yard, 1946: deep-green lacquer walls, emerald curtains and slip covers. The Korean screen and English clock are black-and-gold lacquer.

lacquer screen glistening with gold. The floor is bare, except for some small fur rugs, and the furniture covered with cream-colored raw silk. Those brass bookcases are children of the ones I designed for Cole Porter's apartment in the Waldorf Towers. The Roman shades at the windows are made of dark-brown raw silk, and the mirrors are hung in strategic places to catch all the sparkle of New York at night.

1973: I found myself at home more in the day, and my room had to wake up. I pushed the furniture around so the sofa would catch the afternoon sun, replaced the rather stuffy felt-covered writing table with an airier one of wrapped willow and black glass, and added a few more bits of mirror (the mirror in the room has multiplied steadily over the years—eventually the whole apartment may be lined with it). The only other furniture I added are two small tables of gun-metal Lucite. The pictures are also new: four strong black-and-white drawings by Al Held, and a big black-and-white abstract by Edward Corbett in the bed alcove. Gone from the apartment is all the old clutter. What you see are absolute necessities plus a few treasured objects. Everything else has gone to auction.

The major change was again color. The walls are exactly the same—that color really is for life—but the floor is now covered wall to wall with a white carpet of a rather lineny texture, although it is really wool. The furniture is slip-covered in a marvelous white linen and cotton from Nantucket Looms that has very much the texture of the carpeting, an effect that pleases me because it smooths out the room and calms things down. The dark-brown Roman shades were replaced with spanking-new creamy glazed chintz—a brightening change that has made all the difference between night and day.

Amster Yard, 1951: white with yellow Siamese silk. Above the sofa, those brilliant icy-red apples

Amster Yard, 1955: the entire room is sheathed in white brocade, but the furniture arrangement hasn't changed a bit. New painting above the sofa: English hounds from the early-eighteenth century

Midtown, 1963: opposite page, and left, *the Coromandel-brown room, with the hounds and lacquer screen from Amster Yard, and brand-new brass bookcases. The writing table is covered in brown felt to the floor, which is bare.*

Midtown, 1973: same walls, same bookcases (only more of them). Felt table has been replaced with airy rattan, floor spread wall to wall with lineny white wool.

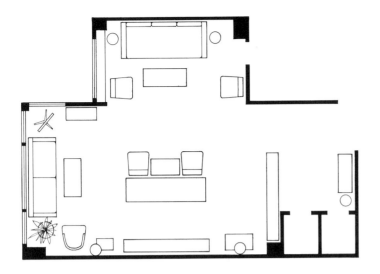

In 1973 I moved the sofa to the window where the table had been, put the table in front of a bookcase. The bed alcove makes a cozy little sitting room. The little armless slipper chairs can be pulled around where they are needed most.

Midtown, 1973: dark-brown Roman shades were replaced with cream-colored glazed chintz. Above the Louis XV armchair hang drawings by Al Held. Opposite: the lord of the manor in his mirrored domain. Black-and-white abstract is by Edward Corbett; small pale gouaches by Paul Feeley.

CHAPTER 12

Stars in My Crown

Mrs. William McCormick Blair, Jr.

Deeda Blair, an up-to-date woman with charmingly old-fashioned manners, has succeeded in adapting the eighteenth century of France to suit herself, adding to its opulence the comforts of today. Her insistence upon excellence is uncompromising, and she will wait indefinitely for just the right thing rather than accept second best. Deeda does all her own flowers, too—selects them one by one and fixes them with patience and love; Heaven help the florist who tries to sneak in with an "arrangement."

The Blairs' whole house is light and luminous. Even the library is painted not dark but bony-white, with an overscaled Okada in blues and greens that echoes in Japanese abstract the treetops and sky of Washington beyond the library terrace.

Deeda is shown standing on that very terrace, looking, in her dark Givenchy dress, like a deep anemone against the sylvan background.

Stark Young

No one ever wrote so sympathetically about the South, or with such dazzling perception. His novels—*Heaven Trees, River House*, and the best-selling *So Red the Rose*—were sources of profound pleasure to me when I lived in Baltimore, as was his drama criticism in the *New Republic* and the New York *Times*. And when I came to live in New York, I had the privilege of his friendship as well.

I remember when Stark was translating Chekhov's *The Sea Gull* for Alfred Lunt and Lynn Fontanne. On long weekends during that spring he would lean back against a gnarled old apple tree covered with white blossoms and read me page after page of his translation. The wonder of it was that, since Stark knew little more than the basics of Russian, the translation was being done mostly by sound and rhythm. The next winter he took me to the New York opening. It was then that I understood his rapport with Chekhov. The first act of *The Sea Gull* might just as well have taken place in one of those lazy country houses in Maryland, where I grew up.

Stark lived in one of the most memorable houses I have ever known. Outside, it was a gray-shingled eighteenth-century salt box; inside, the walls were whitewashed, the woodwork lacquered white, and the floors unfinished and scrubbed like butcher blocks. The furniture was simple and bold, the pictures big and black and Italian. There were towering bouquets of garden and field flowers—or sometimes a single perfect rose in a glass bottle, very Zurbarán. The house showed the influence of William McKnight Bowman, Stark's great friend and perhaps the most sensitive architect I have ever known.

Opposite: *Mrs. William McCormick Blair, Jr.*   *Stark Young*

The food Stark served in that salt box was an experience in itself; a delectable combination of Italy and the American South.

Mrs. T. Reed Vreeland

Diana Vreeland, I am certain, could live forever on her senses alone, so rich are the delicacies they provide. She is opulent and sensuous, stimulating and romantic. She has an uncommonly discerning eye, and her taste defies definition. The times have always had to rush to keep up with Diana.

She was for years responsible for *Vogue*'s appetizing pages that brought me from the humdrum to a feast almost too rich to be digested. She has since designed a breathtakingly beautiful Balenciaga parade and a fashion exhibition called "Inventive Clothing," both for the Metropolitan Museum of Art.

Diana is tireless. Working with her is like being at a fantastic party. One Sunday when Diana and her husband, Reed, and I were going over the plans for their apartment, Diana suddenly stood up and said: "I want this room to be a garden—but a garden in hell."

I knew what that meant: *red*. I searched for an eternity before I found exactly the right material—in John Fowler's shop in London. It was a scarlet chintz with brilliant Persian flowers. I raced home with yards and yards of it and we covered the whole room—walls, curtains, furniture, the works. Diana's apartment has since been described by Charles Beistegui, that influential Parisian style setter, as "the most complete dwelling in New York." Here you see Diana, like a *tulipe noire*, in the midst of her fire and brimstone.

Cole Porter

Cole Porter was abroad when I completed my work on his apartment in the Waldorf Towers (Truman Capote was later to write that I had "transformed it into an island of sublime and subtle luxury"). When Cole stepped through the door of Apartment 33A for the first time, he just looked around in amazement.

"Is this all mine?" he asked.

It all was. He had inherited everything from his wife, Linda, who had lovingly collected every bit of the beautiful French furniture in Paris before the war. Cole had lived with it for years, scarcely aware of it. Now that it all belonged to him, he felt a responsibility. "In order to really possess your possessions," he said to me, "you must know and understand them."

Right after he moved in, he pasted up two charts side by side on his shaving mirror: one of English kings, one of French kings, both dating from the seventeenth

Cole Porter

century. That was the start of his education. He learned quickly, and grew to be very knowledgeable about his treasures. He was proud of them not as status symbols, but for the very fine things they were.

Cole was one of the bravest men I have ever known. He lived a great part of his life in agony, his legs having been crushed in a riding accident on Long Island. Yet he went on creating joyous music. He seemed sometimes to be living in two dimensions at once, slipping easily back and forth between his private world of inspiration and the lower realm known to the rest of us. In the midst of a conversation, he would suddenly drift off, and you could tell by his eyes that he had left you. Here, Cole has been captured in his other world: a close-up of him far away. What delicious melody is he hearing? What lyric, sad or gay?

Van Day Truex

The highest praise Van Day Truex can give any work of art, music, or interior design is the one simple phrase, which he pronounces dramatically: "It is a statement." He has demanding tastes, unswerving integrity, great sensitivity. He believes in simplicity and in sincerity—and he lives that way.

Van graduated from the Paris branch of the Parsons School of Design, and eventually became the head of the entire institution. Under his leadership Parsons blossomed into a brilliant place of learning, where students had not only the chance to see all the great museum rooms, but also an invaluable entree into the best houses and apartments in New York and the neighboring countryside, where real life went on. I had the privilege of lecturing at Parsons during his reign, and the vitality of the whole place was positively energizing.

As soon as Van became associated with Tiffany's, he saw to it that the same kind of inspired transformation took place. Out went the stuffiness of bygone days; in came the fresh innovative designs of the best contemporary artists in the world.

Van attacks everything he undertakes with tremendous energy and seriousness. Yet he has the most delightful sense of humor, complete and unabridged.

Ina Claire (Mrs. William Wallace)

When I was a very young man in Baltimore, I saw Ina Claire in a play called *Polly with a Past*. She was brilliantly clever, and wore a dress the color of flame. I had never before known the meaning of the word glamour.

Her last appearance on Broadway was in *The Confidential Clerk* and I saw that, too. She was just as brilliant and just as glamorous, but perhaps deeper—less actress, more woman.

Van Day Truex

Miss Ina Claire

Whitney Warren with me

Baroness Philippe de Rothschild

Between these two events, I came to know Ina. She asked Ruby Ross Wood to help with the decoration of a flat she had taken, and I was assigned to work with her closely. She was, it is true, a nonstop talker, but it was also true that she had wonderful taste—in decoration as well as clothes. When she chose materials for slip covers or curtains, she would parade back and forth in front of a looking glass—talking the whole time—holding the sample behind her head to see what the colors would do to her skin tones. When we shopped for furniture, she literally charged at things she liked (mostly Regency, which suited her well), grabbing them up in her arms. She loved to shop so much that often we got back to the office long after it had closed. I would be collapsing with fatigue, but Ina was as sparkling and energetic as if it were midday. And she never stopped talking.

In the middle of our work on the apartment, Ina was called to Hollywood to play the Grand Duchess in *Ninotchka*, which also starred Greta Garbo and Melvyn Douglas. What a witty performance she gave! What style! Needless to say, it was a talkie. . . .

Whitney Warren

Whitney Warren is quite simply the most civilized man in San Francisco. He knows how to live. He works on weekends for the museum and the opera, which he loves, and entertains dazzlingly in his exciting apartment at the top of Telegraph Hill. During the week, he goes out to his ranch near Sacramento, on which he lives in the little Basque house you see us in here and which produces the finest peaches and almonds to be had anywhere. In spring, his gardens burst forth with camellias, then tree peonies, and then roses of every color and size imaginable.

There is a special depth to Whitney that resists definition, that reveals itself in unexpected ways. One day, walking through his thickly carpeted acres of chickweed, we came to a great field of rich soft earth planted with rows of tiny trees; they were barely more than leafing twigs stuck in their little mounds.

"These are my new pear trees," Whitney said with pride. "Just planted this year."

"How beautiful they will be when they are grown," I said.

"Yes, they *will* be beautiful." And he smiled. "But they are very slow growers, and I will not live to see them."

Baroness Philippe de Rothschild

When Pauline Potter was seventeen and living in Baltimore, she told me: "This is the most charming city in the world to make your debut in. But when a girl is married, she must go to live in New York. And after that, she must live the whole rest of her life in France, married to a Frenchman."

It sounded like so much daydreaming at the time, but the extraordinary thing is that it has all happened exactly as she planned. With rigid self-discipline, she has cultivated in herself one of the world's finest specimens of civilized humanity.

Of all the women I have ever known, Pauline has the surroundings that are—and always have been—the most personal. There is never *ever* the sense of a decorator's intrusion, and I acknowledge with pride that she has the taste and creativity any decorator could envy. She lives in an ambience of romance and intellect: her houses, her clothes, her food, her flowers and table decorations are all designed to be comforts not only for the body, but also for the mind.

Baltimore's fairest debutante, Pauline is shown wearing a pale-pink fox-furred jacket over a big black taffeta skirt—the costume she often wore to the Garretts' chamber music concerts at Evergreen House. Then, as always, everyone adored her for her charming manners, her sparkling wit, her laughter as light and effortless as sunshine.

Mrs. William S. Paley

She might have been painted by Boldini, or by Picasso in his Rose Period. So great is her beauty that no matter how often I see her, each time is the first time.

She is the essence of the chic and sophisticated woman, yet inside is a delightful little girl who every so often bubbles to the surface—she can become giddy with excitement over the planting of a new garden.

Barbara Paley leads the most demanding life with seeming effortlessness and charming sincerity. Her humor springs from her heart, making all the people she knows want to open their hearts to her. And they do! There is no more sympathetic listener.

Here she stands in her former apartment at the St. Regis filled with hotel furniture made magically her own with miles of Indian cotton as slip covers and, gathered like a tent, on the pictureless walls. She contributed the blackamoor-bordered needlepoint carpet and the quixotic chandelier, as well as clusters of objects all lovingly hers.

In dreams, I see Barbara in a lofty white contemporary room, with soft furniture in white, blue, brown. Kabuki!

Mrs. William S. Paley

Mrs. Harding Lawrence

One of the wonders of Mary Wells Lawrence is that she knows her own style so well. When I saw her for the first time, she was from head to toe as golden and glowing as a sheaf of wheat. And that is the way I shall always think of her.

Mary knows her life style perfectly, too, as so few others do who live varied and exciting lives; she knows how she wants to live and how she wants to feel when she's at home. Her message to me came through loud and clear: all the houses were to be harbors of peace and beauty to sail into after the rigors of a superhuman workday.

The greatest gift the Lawrences ever gave me was their trust. They have never suffered a moment's indecision. They are boldly intelligent, unspoiled, open, and appreciative. They are the ultimate flowering and fulfillment of a decorator's dream.

Mrs. Harding Lawrence

Mrs. Thomas Bancroft

Mrs. Thomas Bancroft

Missy Bancroft has the silken look of a tawny young lioness—but her laughter is more a kitten's purr. Her house in the country is the delight of her life, and filled with light and joy. Fires burn in every room; the house rings with the sounds of her three children; beloved dogs scamper about, members of the family, too. On the walls hang photographs and paintings of the Bancrofts' own horses and the famous horses that Tommy Bancroft's grandfather raced. Always there is the freshness and fragrance of flowers.

Here, Missy is in the living room that the Bancrofts added to the house they love so much; she has made it a haven and a treat for her family as well as her guests.

Mrs. Thomas Kempner

No matter how many people are in a room, my eye is immediately stopped by the same outstanding woman: tall, good-looking, extremely *racée*. She is outshone by neither her clothes nor her surroundings. She is Nan Kempner.

Here, Nan sits, dressed by Yves St. Laurent, in her small library. This is the room where she and her family do most of their living. Here, too, gather the guests for her midweek mixed lunches—memorable for the esoteric food and fascinating talk.

This library is one of those rooms that seem to grow like a garden. The upholstered furniture has been here since Nan came to New York as a bride from San Francisco twenty-four years ago. The room has seen many slip covers, but the furniture itself is everlasting. The room is everlasting, too; Nan may add a picture or a small table, or introduce an object or a beautiful flowering plant, but the room has never undergone a radical change. Nan Kempner tends her garden with care. I watched her once as she arranged some Chinese porcelains she had just inherited. She handled the treasures with great sensuousness and calm, slowly, almost ritualistically. I felt as if I were intruding on a very intimate moment in her life.

Outside, the city is changing, changing. But it is comforting to know that no matter how far or how long you have been away, Nan Kempner's library will be there, timeless, waiting to welcome you home.

Señora de Don Placido Arango

Thank heaven the Arangos stopped long enough in New York, when they were moving from Mexico back to Spain, to ask if I would consider the faraway job of an apartment in Madrid. That was the start of one of the happiest relationships I've ever had with a client.

The Arangos' apartment is smack in the middle of Madrid. You can throw a stone and hit the Prado, another and hit the Ritz. The Arangos wanted a bright, country atmosphere for their three beautiful children, so we gave the apartment the look of a country house, very light and breezy, with lovely old furniture from England and France.

Maité Arango herself is very like the apartment we created: quiet in voice and manner, yet brimming over with joy. She is shown standing like a serene calla lily at the doors that open from the drawing room to the terrace overlooking the charming old pink tile roofs of the Botanical Gardens.

Mrs. Thomas Kempner

Señora de Don Placido Arango   Opposite: *Mrs. Frederick Melhado*

Mrs. Frederick Melhado

Louise Melhado is as feminine as a flower. And she is always surrounded by flowers: flowers on her dresses, in her decoration, and fresh flowers by the armful. Everything about her—her voice, her clothes, the way she moves—is petal soft; even her laughter is like a thing in bloom. But be careful, her wit is like a pale-green thorn—not without a sting.

She is the best housekeeper of any young woman I know. To be her house guest is to be treated to every comfort imaginable—and some you never did imagine. The guest room is a bower of luxury. And Louise has an uncanny knack for serving just the food you've been longing for.

Here, she sits quite properly on the floor in a caftan amid a bouquet of Moroccan pillows: the supreme combination of stripes and flowers.

CHAPTER 13

Thorns in My Crown

"HOW WONDERFUL IT MUST BE," my dinner partner is likely to begin, "to spend all your time dreaming up beautiful places for beautiful people to live in."

And it's true, of course. Creating and arranging beautiful things for fascinating people is the delight of a decorator's life—and I give thanks that mine has been filled with it. But there is the heartbreaking side of decorating, too—hair-tearing episodes without which no memoir would be complete and, worse, no delights measured.

A decorator contends, on the one hand, with The Industry.

Item: A workman has just installed the faceplates on all the electric wall sockets in a remodeled house. Astonishingly, without exception, they all tilt between twenty and thirty degrees off the vertical. "These must be straightened at once," I say, reasonably enough. "The painters are coming in the morning." The man looks at his watch. "Too late," he says, shrugging helplessly. "Quitting time."

Item: Two upholsterers are working side by side on a pair of matching chairs. One concentrates on his work, obviously enjoying it, proud of doing his very best. The other smokes his cigarette, makes small talk with passers-by, scarcely pays attention to his chair. He seems to find perverse pleasure in being able to get away with shoddy workmanship. Their union rules decree, however, that both these men must be paid the same hourly wage.

Item: I take my manufacturer's sample of a heavenly beige raw silk and go to claim the hundred yards of it I ordered several months ago. After much searching through records and bundles, the man presents me with one hundred yards of taupe-colored cotton-and-rayon. "But this is nothing at all like the sample," I say, wanting to weep (three months of waiting for a piece of cloth and then finding it totally unacceptable has brought my most primitive emotions to the surface). "You'll be a nervous wreck if you take things so hard," the man says to console me. "Take the stuff. Your client will never know the difference."

On the other hand, the decorator must also contend with The Client—and although they are mostly nice little girls grown up, some are decidedly lacking in sugar and spice.

You see some of them in the Third Avenue markets, joyless and grim on the arms of their sentenced decorators, seeking not loveliness but status symbols. There are clients for whom uniqueness is an absolute necessity: anything that has ever been thought of before is ex officio unacceptable. There are others so timid they won't accept anything they *haven't* seen done; if you count on one eccentric table or chair to lift the scheme out of its banality, you can be sure that's just the thing they will insist that you have removed.

If nothing pleases one client, everything pleases another to the point of rapture—but she never gets around to making up her mind. And when it's all over and the room is done, who do you think takes responsibility for the brilliant decoration if the lady is satisfied? And if she is not, who do you think gets blamed?

Some of the thorns in my crown are more prickly than others, of course. Some are painful, others merely preposterous; some are ludicrous, others just incredible. This is not to imply that we decorators do not also commit sins of our own. But those are thorns in *your* crown. . . .

Billy Rose, Napoleon of Broadway

"There's a Mr. Billy Rose on the telephone," Miss Schwick, my secretary, announced one Friday morning. I picked up the receiver.

"Yes, Mr. Rose," I said.

"Hello, Billy Baldwin, the name's not Mr. Rose, it's Billy Rose," boomed the voice on the other end. "And I've just bought the finest house in New York, built and lived in by William Goadby Loew." My interest was aroused; one could not possibly exaggerate the architectural merits of the Loew house. "I'm a very busy man," the voice continued, and I could tell that it was accustomed to command. "Meet me there tomorrow morning."

I glanced at my calendar: Saturday was blissfully clear. But I couldn't pass this up.

I got to the house early, and was admitted by a caretaker to an entrance hall of perfect proportions. The room was barren of furniture, and every sound had an overlapping echo. At the appointed hour, an immense Rolls-Royce pulled up to the curb, and down from the driver's seat climbed little Billy Rose—a man, I was pleased to note, who was even shorter than I. His pretty wife was with him, a fact he hardly seemed to be aware of as we shook hands all around and began our tour.

Billy Rose talked the best taste imaginable. It was obvious he had seen a good deal of the world and knew the difference between value and junk. "I want this to have the atmosphere of one of those stately homes of England," he thundered as we passed through one room after another—all, I might add, equally impressive. I found, as his heels clicked a staccato rhythm across the beautiful parquet floors, that his enthusiasm was contagious.

I began suggesting various room plans, furniture arrangements, and ideas for structural changes as they occurred to me, even possible colors. When we came to the huge dining room, I had an instant vision of just how it could look. "Why not put a sofa and chairs over near the window?" I suggested.

"Wonderful!" he exclaimed. "Just like they do in England. And the drawing room

152

naturally will be all French—the best money can buy. There'll be a couple of Nattiers, too," he said, his voice lowering to a confidential blare. "I know where I can get them for nothing."

My eyebrows arched involuntarily. "I can get other pictures for nothing, too," he bragged. "Gainsborough, Reynolds, Romney—I'm going to bring back to fashion the eighteenth-century art of England."

I noticed that Mrs. Rose was not consulted about anything, even the decorating plans for her own bedroom. Once or twice, when she ventured to whisper a tentative thought, she was told matter-of-factly to shut up. She should have known better; this was a Billy Rose production.

After a couple of hours of this, he began to talk hard business. "Now I want you to start at once," he commanded. "You will be put on a retainer, just like my attorneys, and, just like them, you will be available to me twenty-four hours a day." This meant that if, for instance, he heard that some special breakfront he was looking for was available in London, I was to drop everything and fly over with him. Furthermore, I could expect to be awakened for these trips in the middle of the night; Billy Rose wanted to be in London in the morning. I would then have to stand by while he bargained with the seller (bargaining, I gathered, was his favorite sport) until the "ridiculous" price got down to a level he considered reasonable.

He apparently expected my answer on the spot. "I'm overwhelmed," I told him, rather meekly, "but I really have to think about it. The house is obviously going to take a good deal of my time, and it might interfere with my other clients."

"You won't need any other clients for several years," he bellowed reassuringly. "I'm going to make you so famous you'll push the Suez Canal right off the front page of the *Times*." His enthusiasm was peaking again. "This house," he said, "is going to be the greatest thing ever done in New York. It'll be even better than the Wallace Collection in London—not only will it be top quality, but it'll be livable." Quivering with excitement, he told me I could even wear colored shirts if I wanted to. He would make them famous and have me acclaimed as the best-dressed man in America. He slapped my shoulder affably and left, air rushing to fill the vacuum where he had just been.

Billy Rose couldn't have made a bigger impression on me if he had run me over with his Rolls-Royce. I rushed home, pumping adrenaline all the way, to recover with a Campari and soda and a telephone call to my calm partner, Edward Martin. I knew perfectly well the whole idea was preposterous. For a decorator to abandon his entire clientele for a single job, however grand and well paying, is very poor policy indeed, and especially questionable in this case, where there seemed to be so many unconventional fringe benefits. The problem was how to tell a steam roller of a man like Billy Rose. I knew I wouldn't get anywhere trying to refuse him to his face.

Edward and I decided the best thing would be for me to write a note saying the prospect was enticing but impossible because of my current work load.

As soon as the note went out by messenger the first thing Monday morning, I was back in real life again and off to Philadelphia for the opening of *The Reluctant Debutante*, for which I had designed the sets. I spent ten grueling hours working in the theatre and it was after midnight when I dropped at last onto my hotel bed.

Just as I was drifting off, the telephone beside me jangled. A screaming voice crackled from the earpiece—I jerked my head away reflexively.

"How dare you leave New York without telling me?" demanded the voice, a tidal wave even at six inches away. I could feel the telephone wires humming all the way from New York.

"Mr. Rose . . ." I began.

"The name's Billy Rose, Billy Baldwin," he interrupted. "And I want to know which train you're going to be on in the morning. I want you to come straight to my office from Penn Station." He called me every category of fool, revealing, by the way, a marked deficiency in the English language. I deduced that since Saturday morning he had considered me as good as under contract to him; he was accustomed to having people tied with ribbons and delivered to his door. I forgave my staff for telling him where I was staying—no one could resist that force for long.

When he was through, I said in my quietest voice: "Mr. Rose, I had a lovely morning with you and your charming wife at your new house. Your enthusiasm was wonderful and I got so caught up by it that I gave you valuable advice for nothing. However, my note stands. I am simply too busy to accept your offer. Now, if you will excuse me, it is very late, and I am very tired, and I wish to say thank you for considering me, good night and good-by." The telephone went dead in my ear.

Some months later I saw him again, quite by chance, as he was stepping from an elevator.

"Hello, Billy Baldwin," he said, smiling broadly. "Still too busy?"

"How are you, Mr. Rose?" I said.

"The name's *Billy Rose!*" he roared, and walked off.

The Eye Not Fooled Enough

"Now don't get excited," said the soft, slightly Southern voice of a very well known widow who was calling to have me come and see her. "It's just a small job."

I got excited anyway, of course. I had seen her in her palace on Park Avenue years before when Ruby Ross Wood was working on her bedroom and took me along to see the house. The Spanish patio that now takes up a colossal room in the Metropolitan Museum was then comfortably installed there.

Even before that, I had known of the lady: back in Baltimore, everyone talked about a certain beauty who had married well and gone to live in New York. So the prospect of seeing her again, of working for her this time, was doubly intriguing. She received me looking very handsome indeed. "I know you come from Baltimore," she said warmly, "but did you know I do, too? But I came from the wrong side of the tracks." I was totally disarmed.

The reason for my being there was a long rather boring hallway leading to the bedrooms. It was full of awkward doors and painted common apartment-house cream. But there was treasure here: six beautiful drawings by Tiepolo, although they looked rather lonesome and forlorn in that gloomy hall.

It didn't take me long to cook up a plan. There was no room for furniture in the narrow passageway, but the Tiepolos made up for that. What they needed was, first of all, some decent light, and, second, a beautiful subtle background—nothing overpowering, just something to hang comfortably on. I suggested a *trompe-l'oeil* treatment with marbleized walls and moldings on the many doors so that they would become a part of the decoration. Light would be provided by simple unobtrusive spots recessed in the ceiling.

My client was delighted with the little sketch I gave her and approved the plan. Then she packed up for her annual summer in Europe. Just as she was leaving—she was practically out the door—she asked me to replace all the lamp shades in the living room, library, and her bedroom. I was to have everything done by the time she returned in the fall.

The first thing I did was employ the best artist in New York to do the *trompe-l'oeil*. It took him all summer—the detail was painstaking. But when he was done, it was a masterpiece.

While he was busy in the hall, I was measuring all the lamps for their new shades. There must have been two dozen of them, but I couldn't have agreed more that they needed to be replaced. The rooms were crowded with museum-quality French furniture, eighteenth-century paintings, and extraordinary carpets—none of which could be seen. All the lamp shades were dingy silk pagodas or other distorted shapes elaborately trimmed with fringes and tassels. The light they gave can only be described as dirty. I replaced them all with simple shades of off-white paper edged with thin gold bands. All the insides were painted a barely visible blush pink to soften the light. They made a lovely difference: the rooms now glowed.

Finally, the hallway lighting was completed, the Tiepolos rehung (how very much at home they looked in their new Italianate setting), and summer was over.

In no time I was summoned by the lady. Again she looked beautiful, refreshed by her summer abroad. But she was rather cool as she led me to the hallway entrance.

"Mr. Baldwin," she said, "I always heard not only that you have lovely taste, but that you are very efficient as well and can be counted on to have everything done by the promised date." She paused, waiting for me to say something. But I had all I could do trying to fathom what on earth she was driving at. "When," she continued, "are you going to do the work?"

I was stunned. I took her hand and led her down the hall, gesturing at the beautiful details. "The work," I said, "is done."

She looked all around, and sighed heavily. "Well, I accepted your charming little sketch and your estimate, which seemed rather a lot," she said. "And for all that, I see no difference."

I didn't know what to say. The whole point of the decoration was its subtlety.

"As for those lamp shades," she went on, "please call for them at the earliest possible moment. Thank heaven my maid saved the old ones."

"The lamp shades!" I exclaimed, dumfounded. "What can possibly be wrong with *them*?"

"Mr. Baldwin," she admonished, "no lady would ever have paper lamp shades."

The Unfinished Symphony

The voice on the telephone had a beguiling foreign accent. It belonged to the wife of a famous American composer-conductor, and an actress in her own right. "I want to begin by telling you that I have always been my own decorator," she said. "But I'm stuck. Will you help me?"

I went to see her the very next day. Their apartment was attractive, although I must say there were some blatant borrowings from the tastes of well-known decorators. However, she pulled everything together nicely and the rooms were filled with wonderful memorabilia, mostly from her husband's varied and successful career.

The problem was the dining room. It was to be used entirely for parties, principally for the after-concert suppers the couple was fond of giving. But, she told me, there must also be a quiet place for her husband to have breakfast and read the morning paper.

I envisioned a ravishing room. It is not often that a decorator is given the chance to do a room meant for pleasure only, where price is obviously no object, where the only thing that matters is that everything be first class and madly beautiful. I fairly licked my chops in anticipation.

I saw that the architecture of the room was perfect for a pair of banquettes, each with a large round table. There was a nice long wall for a buffet, and two windows in the southeast corner—a warm sunny place for a small breakfast table and a comfortable chair.

I worked out the details back at my office. For sound control: flannel-backed cloth stretched across the walls, plus beautiful wall-to-wall carpeting. For extra seating with the banquettes: a set of chairs— I knew where I could get twelve super black-and-gold-painted Regency armchairs in London. For excitement: mirrors—two spectacular ones were available abroad that would provide just the sparkle the room needed. This was going to be a spectacular room, just right for its purpose, just right for its owners, and a glittering setting for all the glamorous people I knew would fill it. I was very excited, and sent the plans and estimates over right away.

The telephone rang early the next morning.

"It's a dream of beauty, and just perfect," said Madame's lovely voice. "But the cost—we were absolutely floored. Neither of us could sleep last night."

I apologized, trying as best I could to conceal my disappointment. I was puzzled —the price was fair and certainly not out of hand for them. They had not even given me a budget. "I realize the room is expensive," I said. "But it never occurred to me that you would tolerate anything less than the very best in quality, design, or workmanship. None of that comes cheap." There was a fluttery sound and a few whispers, and the conductor himself came to the telephone.

"We think your plan is beautiful," he said, "but the price is absurd." It was obvious he was going to try to bargain with me. But lowering the price would have meant changing something major: omitting the wall covering or the banquettes, or using common little chairs instead of the ones I had in mind for them. The perfection of the room was that everything went together, and no detail was unessential.

I hesitated, and then I spoke. "If someone asked you to write a score," I said, "and it turned out exactly the way you wanted it—everything fitting together so that not a thing was superfluous, nor another thing needed—and then that someone asked you to change it, what would you do?"

There was a pause.

"You're right, Mr. Baldwin," he said. "I wouldn't change a single note."

We never spoke again.

Love's Labour's Lost

Imagine my excitement when I was asked to decorate a whole triplex penthouse newly bought by a theatre director so astonishing he had four smash hits running at the same time on Broadway and a movie that was breaking box-office records everywhere. The director took me to his apartment himself, proud and enthusiastic. I knew we could work well together.

On the main floor of the apartment was the entrance hall, with a dining room on one side, a library on the other, and a big living room ringed by a narrow balcony. A staircase led up to a bed-bath-dressing suite, which opened onto a vast rooftop terrace.

From the bedroom a circular staircase wound up inside a tower to a sitting room with spectacular arched windows.

Because the life of a director meant late to bed, late to rise, the bedroom had to be enormously comfortable and protected from the morning sun. The dining room had to be flexible enough for all kinds of dining—small parties, large ones, casual or formal entertaining. The handsome square library was to be used as an office at home, a cozy room where the director could receive business callers and do much of his afternoon work. The little tower room was to be strictly a personal retreat—an escape from Broadway. But the big downstairs living room was to be glamour: used exclusively for parties—a glittery, star-studded New York Room. The director and I agreed on everything. The partnership was perfect.

I decided to capitalize on the living room's expanses of windows facing south and east and give the room the look of the outdoors. The walls were painted and glazed the color of straw; a real straw carpet covered most of the beigey terrazzo floor; and a pair of enormous sofas by the fire were covered in straw-colored linen patterned with white Chinese vases (a material designed by David Hicks, who used the same pattern in blue and white in his own country house in England). Between the two sofas stood a big square coffee table of natural-colored lacquered raffia. In the east window we set up a card table and four chairs—nice for lunches or little dinners for four—of wrapped willow and waterproof leather the color of sand. There were some wood pieces, notably a simple Louis XVI commode, and a dozen small chairs upholstered in honey-colored suède, to be arranged at will. And, of course, there was an endlessly long black concert grand piano. Everywhere stood huge tall plants, with spotlights shining up through their branches. We left the big beautiful windows entirely curtainless, but I knew we would need some protection from sun and glare. I hit upon a classical solution: awnings lined with canvas the color of the Mediterranean Sea. In the daytime, the view from the sofas was like an ocean-beach landscape of golden sand, sky, and sea. At night, the awnings were rolled up and out of sight, and all you could see were the stars. And when you got up and walked to the window, there was that beautiful view down the length of Manhattan—a sight that never fails to justify one's living there.

To this day I think of that room, out of all the hundreds I have designed, as the one that appealed to me most of all. But, alas, the client is the ultimate court of appeals.

Within a week he was on the telephone, asking me to come see him. Something in his voice told me that our perfect partnership was no more. He took me to the big room, which I must say looked particularly ravishing flooded with afternoon sunshine.

"I cannot make myself feel at home in this room," my client began softly. "I just never want to come in here. It has nothing to do with me."

"But I don't ever want you to come in here alone," I told him. "I want you to look in at it, and see that you have a thing of beauty. When it is filled with people, I want you to see how it comes to life." I told the director that the room was like a beautiful piece of jewelry—precious, but not for every day.

"I have a very good friend whose taste I have complete faith in," he continued, "and she doesn't like the room at all." I shivered. Other People's Opinions are the death knell to a decorator's work.

"You have a wonderful cozy library that you love," I pointed out, almost pleading with him. "You have a fireplace and a seating group in your bedroom, and another cozy sitting room up in the tower where you can be alone or with close friends. *This* room is meant for drama, for entertaining, for sparkle. Won't you just give one single party in it to see how wonderful it is?"

"No," he said, shaking his head. "My mind is made up. I'll pay for everything, of course. But this room has got to go. I'm starting over." I sighed. It was just too special, I suppose, for Broadway.

I got into his elevator and descended to the street, my heart breaking. Recently, I saw a play he directed—not with the tough popular humor of his former work, but with the greatest subtlety and sensitivity. I know a man like that would soon have come to understand and love that room that he destroyed.

The Pound of Flesh

The day began like any other. A woman came into my office to discuss a country house she was building. She was a woman of unquestionable intelligence, a Broadway producer, in fact, and linked by both blood and marriage to the highest echelons of Hollywood.

But, instead of discussing the house and its decoration, she launched into a long description of the glorious Hollywood house she had once shared with her late movie-producer husband. She talked until *my* throat was dry, skillfully deflecting my every attempt to discuss the business at hand.

"Won't you come to my apartment for dinner tonight?" she asked as the morning drew to an end. "We can talk at length then." I try to avoid this kind of business-social relationship, but we had accomplished nothing the whole morning, and I certainly did not want to waste half of another business day with her.

Her apartment was handsome but rather sterile, full of beautiful English furniture. There was a small but good-looking kitchen with an atmosphere of intimidating efficiency, and I wondered if a meal consisting of real food could actually be produced there. In the living room, over a cocktail, I broached the subject of country houses, but the lady preferred to tell me the story of her life. It was a very dramatic tale, and her tears, splashing on the floor, were evidence that one of us, at least, found it deeply moving.

During dinner, we finally got around to discussing her new house—or, rather, she did. I was given a long, very complicated description of the sort of atmosphere she wanted to create. There was no possible way to make head or tail of any of it, so about halfway through I gave up trying and concentrated on my dinner, which happened to be very good. I was beginning to have serious misgivings about the whole enterprise, but I decided to go with her in the morning to see the house, and trust to my decorator's instincts about how it could be done to please us both.

The house, which had been designed by one of my favorite architects, was well under way on a charming piece of land through which ran a pretty little river. The beams and studs were up, most of them, and walking from room to room we could get a good feel of the space. I was surprised to see my client display not a trace of the joy and excitement that normally afflict people when they build. Instead, she went to the building site every day in the most irritable mood, policing the workmen and generally spreading her gloom. Perhaps she was wondering if she could have gotten a better house, with a few changes here and there. She trusted no one—least of all the architect himself—and was always trying to alter the plans. Once, she decided a wall should be moved a foot to enlarge a room. The contractor protested, of course, but she created such a scene that at last he gave in. The result was that when he followed the rest of the architect's plans, the roof didn't fit.

She was no better, I found, when it came to the interior. Her idea of making the decoration personal was to have everything absolutely unlike anything she had ever seen. Between the living room and the sunroom, she told me, she wanted not a wall but a sort of "divider" from the floor to about a foot below the ceiling. This divider was to contain a fireplace, books, and an upright piano. I had to confess my inability even to conceive of such a thing. And there were plenty of other requests, just about as reasonable.

"I would like to have the sofa covered in a material I've never seen," she said, smiling with delight at the prospect. "Ideally, one that has never ever been made." I asked if she could give me a little hint. "Perhaps," she said, "one that looks like a lovely little sweater crocheted by old ladies." Maybe, I thought to myself, we could have it done by the Woman's Exchange.

The sight of a telephone, she said, was repulsive to her. I recalled from my childhood that horrible vogue of placing dolls on telephones so that their long crinoline skirts could cascade over them. Her final request of the day was to have the lamp shades made of some unusual material—something no one had ever thought of before.

Instinctively, I knew I ought to withdraw at once. I was unsympathetic to everything she said, and I knew that I could never please her. Besides that, she was a time waster and a self-doubter. Yet I stayed with her. Maybe she had a kind of tragic appeal for me. Maybe it was my own ego, which saw her as a challenge to my creative talents and my patience! But the weeks of meetings dragged on into months and still we were getting nowhere. I sent samples by the hundreds, made scores of suggestions, and everything she mulled over, debated, redebated, and ultimately rejected. I went to each successive meeting proportionately less inspired than the time before and left progressively more drained and exhausted. Had God created Adam just for her, I felt sure the woman would have sent him back.

I began to feel that something was the matter with *me*. "Why can't I please her?" I asked Edward Martin in despair. I persuaded him to come with me on my next visit—perhaps then he could tell me why. After several hours of listening to her complaints and misery, we wrenched ourselves away. Edward's face showed genuine alarm.

"You don't know how awful you look," he told me. "I forbid you to have one more meeting with that woman."

This shocked me to my senses. I was not suffering from a lack of creativity. It was she who was afflicted—with terminal indecision complicated by self-doubt. I meanwhile had probably set some sort of endurance record for survival under extreme duress. And, to top it off, I couldn't even send her a bill—after all those months of torture, her name hadn't even gotten on my books.

Some time later, I learned that I had been succeeded by an exceptionally talented young man, totally lacking in professional experience, who worked for her for several months. He was then removed to a peaceful home in the country to recover from a nervous collapse.

"Folie de Grandeur"

By the time I met a certain multimillionheiress, she had already been married many times over and had managed to remain the poorest little richest girl in modern history. Our lives crossed when she became engaged to a man many years her junior— the very first American to join her stable of husbands, up to then an assortment of European titles. The newest candidate was, however, from the oldest of New York families. "At least," she told me, "I am marrying what would be royalty if such a thing existed in America."

The young man was very good-looking, very charming, and very poor. Naturally, the heiress had produced a handsome dowry for him, as she had for each of her husbands. She told me in our first interview that, in addition to the marriage settlement, she would pay for the decoration of a little house of his in the country. I was intrigued, and agreed to go with Prince Charming (the heiress herself was even then too frail to make the hourlong trip in her hearse of a hired car) to have a look at the little château.

After dinner, the lady drew me aside. "I have known you only a few moments," she said, "but already I know exactly what you are. I could never offer you money or jewels. I will just give you something of myself." With that, she brought out from behind her back a slender book, expensively bound, of love poems she herself had written. They turned out to be tacky almost beyond belief—and the volume was signed by its self-indulgent authoress!

The "house in the country" turned out to be not really a house at all, but a converted barn at a rather trafficky crossroads on the edge of a swamp where cows came to cool their ankles in summer. There was electricity, a meager heating system, definitely no air conditioning, and certainly no furniture to speak of. We browsed around looking for ideas, and I must admit the young aristocrat's were far grander than mine. For a bachelor, it really wasn't such a bad little place, but for an heiress . . .

I gathered that she, never having seen it, fancied herself a modern Marie Antoinette in dairymaid guise. Indeed, she had told me how she always dreamed of a bedroom hung with delicate embroidered muslin (she pronounced it "*moos*leen"), preferably from the eighteenth or nineteenth century. I had thought it a really lovely idea. But now that I was here, and could see the livestock and hear the traffic's roar, the idea of embroidered muslin seemed unsuitable. I tried to picture her after her first view of the house in the country. For that matter, I wondered when she intended to come here at all—she hated America and had always lived abroad.

On the way back to New York, the young man produced three little velvet boxes. "I must show you some of my engagement presents," he said. In each box was a pair of cuff links: one pair of diamonds, the next of sapphires, the third of rubies. I mustered my most innocent expression as I gazed at them.

"But look here," I said, "she forgot the emeralds."

"You're quite right!" he said, apparently noticing the omission for the first time. "I shall have to remind her."

A few days later, Prince Charming called to say that his lady fair had let him have forty thousand dollars to decorate his house. Off I went to the country with my usual crew to measure for paint, curtains, rugs, and all the other components that go into transforming a barn into a little palace. I then prepared my plans and mailed my estimates to him. He called immediately.

"I just got these estimates," he said. "You certainly don't expect me to pay them."

"Oh?" I asked. "But I thought you had forty thousand dollars to spend."

"I have better things to do with that money," he said.

"Well, then, do you want me to send the estimates to *her*?"

"Billy," he said with a tone of finality, "I don't care what you do with them."

Now this was an interesting development. I happened to know the lady's broker, so I called to tell him the story.

"Sorry," the broker told me, "but the gentleman already has forty thousand to pay those bills. I'll not allow her to pay another cent."

Before this little situation could be resolved, I was told that my services would not be needed after all; no mention was made of the time and effort I had already spent— odd, in view of all the millions lying about. The engagement had been broken off, and the swamp was left to the cows.

Paradise Lost

I had known the lady playwright and her work. She had quite a reputation among our many mutual friends for brains, beauty, and pretty awful taste. I was also fully aware that she was an outspoken convert to Catholicism.

We were meeting to discuss the decoration of an elaborate triplex she and her magazine-publisher husband had just bought. Her attack—of which I heartily approved —was to tell me the kind of life they planned to lead in the apartment, rather than to dictate decorating ideas.

"I care how it looks, but I do not want to sacrifice efficiency to aesthetics," the lady told me in her businesslike way; I had heard that she was fascinated by gadgetry. "I like to act quickly and I expect you do the same." As she looked at me, her expression changed somehow. "And as soon as you're through with your work, I have to do a little work on you," she said slyly. "You don't realize it yet, but you are already three quarters of the way up the cross—and I am going to give you the final boost."

She and her husband spent weekends at their country house in Connecticut; she asked me to come there for the day so I could get an idea of their taste (my friends were right—it was perfectly awful). The butler who admitted me spoke in a voice hardly more audible than a whisper. I assumed at first there was something the matter with his throat, but I soon came to know that this was the custom among the servants; they were either extremely reverent or utterly terrorized, and I wondered which.

I was led upstairs to a sort of office: an unpleasant, coldly efficient room in which were imprisoned two secretaries with beaten expressions and the same careful, quiet voices. But there was nothing reverent about these two. One of them handed me a bundle of typewritten pages that turned out to be a veritable thesis on the mechanics and gadgetry of the new apartment: there was to be an elaborate intercom telephone system, a complicated arrangement for summoning servants electronically, a great deal of wiring for indirect lighting, considerable reconstruction, and an entirely new kitchen. There was a special note for me: since there was so much room for books in the country house, there would be very few in the city; I was therefore to buy false bookspines for filling in—one of my pet aversions.

In the middle of reading this fascinating treatise I was interrupted by my client, who appeared before me wrapped in a very becoming beach robe.

"It's time for you to swim with me," she announced, not bothering to indulge in the usual exchange of greetings. She led me to the pool and proceeded to do some systematic lapping while I puttered about in the delicious coolness. After about fifteen minutes, she stopped, took a long satisfied breath, and instructed me to get dressed and go tell the secretaries it was their time to swim with her. When I delivered the orders, one of the ladies burst into tears.

"How can she ask us to swim with her?" wailed the other in anguish. "Before you arrived, she was unspeakably cruel to us." But they obeyed.

When their swimming session was over, I was again summoned and we all had a good rich lunch outdoors on the terrace. Madame, I noticed, was having something different—a health salad.

"I hope you all realize," she lectured, "that what you are eating is as nourishing as poison." She was packed with all the facts. But she was extremely dogmatic and wholly lacking in humor, which made conversation with her no great pleasure. Every so often, after a certain amount of concentration, she managed to produce some cheap wisecrack; that was the extent of her wit.

The afternoon schedule called for discussion of decorating plans for the new apartment. There were two rooms that needed special consideration. One was the lady's private sitting room-office, leading from her bedroom. This was to be furnished with a big desk, a great many false bookspines, and a chaise longue from which she could dictate as she reclined.

"I want the room to look like *South Pacific*," she told me. I had no idea what this could mean.

"Perhaps," I suggested facetiously, "we could have sand-colored walls and a blue ceiling and lots of tropical plants."

"You understand perfectly!" she exclaimed.

The other problem room was an enormous drawing room, two stories high, which was to be used primarily for large parties. A piano was a must. And since her husband liked to sit surrounded by his guests, there was a terrific to-do about a special kind of sofa. We finally decided to make it very large and in the shape of a U, and to center it on a long wall between two windows. When the time came to deliver this monster, it had to be hoisted up eighteen floors from the street and swung in through the window.

I suggested that the room be decorated in a rather Venetian style, all pinks and reds, very luxurious and rather jubilant for her glamorous soirées, and she was ecstatic.

Within a few days, all my plans and estimates were ready. I brought them to her hotel myself. The newly hired city butler and maid greeted me at the door—already indoctrinated into the Cult of Whispers. I reacted by saying everything several decibels louder than necessary, and stomping my feet as I walked. They ushered me into the dining room to wait for Madame, who was occupied.

I sat down. An hour and a half later I was still sitting. At last the voices from down the hall grew nearer, and past the open dining-room door walked Madame, beaming, between a handsome young man and a priest. When she had seen them safely to the elevator, she strode into the dining room without a word of apology for having kept me waiting. Instead, she stretched out her arms, palms up, and gazed heavenward. I almost expected to see the stigmata. "Did you see that beautiful young man?" she asked. "Father Kenny brought him to me to say good-by to the world. He is going into the priesthood." Slowly she shook her head. "What a waste."

Work on the apartment progressed with surprising smoothness, in spite of Madame's curious once-a-week "discussions" with the workmen. Promptly at the prearranged hour, she would appear, followed by her entourage of beaten secretaries— one of whom carried a folding chair upon which Her Highness could enthrone herself. The workmen would line up before her.

"Now, plumber," she would say, pointing with her finger at the poor man, "give us your progress report." Loathing glowing in his eyes, he would bring her up to date on the state of copper tubing and privy fixtures. She would nod her head. "Now, electrician," she would say, pointing. And so on, until all work had been accounted for, and all egos reduced to shreds. Finally, she would turn to me and ask, "Do you think they are telling the truth?" Sometimes she would actually get up and walk through the apartment to reassure herself. When she was satisfied, she would say, "Now I shall tell you the state of the world"—and proceed to give us all a little bulletin of current events. These audiences were duly recorded by the two secretaries. After the royal party withdrew, I would have the great pleasure of listening to the workmen's assessment of their employer, which was none too generous, I assure you, and delivered with eloquent simplicity.

Several months later, everything was done. I arranged to meet Madame at the apartment so we could walk through it for the first time together—always an exciting occasion for a decorator and a client. The day before we were to meet, my telephone rang and I recognized the hushed voice of one of the secretaries.

"I know this is less than discreet of me," she whispered, "but I must warn you that Madame visited the apartment secretly yesterday—and she hates the big room."

I was overcome. The room was spectacular—I considered it quite a feather in my cap. And, in any event, it was certainly no surprise to my client. She had seen and approved every single item in it. She had even lived for several weeks with a four-yard length of the damask that now covered the walls. I could not believe she hated the room. Nevertheless, I went to the meeting on my guard. She arrived, glaring at me, her two ladies in waiting right behind her. She wasted no words on pleasantries.

"I loathe everything about this room," she announced, "and I wish you to remove all the furniture by tomorrow."

"I'm sure that can be arranged, Madame," I said, marveling, in my agony, at my self-restraint. "But I'm not sure the sofa hoisters can be scheduled so quickly."

"I will not pay for any special equipment," she said. "Saw the thing in three—it's only suitable for the city dump anyway."

I could no longer contain myself. "I simply cannot understand you," I stormed. "You knew exactly what the room was going to look like, you had the floor plans, you saw and approved every single thing in the entire room, and you loved it all!"

"Well I abhor it now," she said. She strode about the room. "Everything is vulgar and absolutely tasteless. This," she said, pointing to a lovely tufted sofa in the Venetian red velvet she herself had chosen, "looks like Mae West" (her idea of being witty). "I came to you because of your professional reputation," she went on. "But, sir, you are an amateur."

I was stung. The secretaries meanwhile were furiously taking down the whole intercourse in notehand.

"Now," said Madame, "I have no other particular complaints, and I would like to walk through the rest of the apartment with you." We walked, but there was no joy. When we came to the *South Pacific* room, I was startled to see, in the center of it, a tall handsome young priest—winding a clock. Madame's expression softened instantly to one of ardent human kindness. "Isn't it marvelous?" she beamed. "He comes and winds all my clocks—it's therapy."

I left, pulverized. A few days later, after the Venetian room had been dismantled, a little note arrived at my office: "Madame would like the bill as soon as possible, and of course the entire contents of the drawing room should not appear on it." I suppose I could have made a legal case against her, since I had all the signed estimates. But I had not been in business for myself for very long, and I just couldn't face the tedium and expense of a long court battle. I took my loss. Needless to say, I never made it to the top of the cross.

I did, however, see Madame from time to time at large parties—after all, we had many mutual friends and acquaintances (most of whom knew about the disaster because she had made it her Christian business to tell them). I managed successfully to avoid her until a certain New Year's Eve party, the memory of which time cannot erase. At the stroke of midnight, down the long length of the drawing room waltzed Madame herself, giving all the gentlemen a blessing in the form of a kiss. I tried to duck out of the way—too late. Suddenly, we were face to face. A wave of astonishment rippled through the room. With a beatific expression, she leaned forward and kissed me smack on the mouth. Two days later, the blessed spot blossomed with an enormous fever blister—the only one I have ever had in my life.

Honest as the Day Is Long

He was a famous actor of stage and films; she was his charming new Venetian bride, who determined immediately to convert his house into *her* house.

She was delightful, and, more than that, bewitching, although I cannot say her taste and ideas bewitched me that much. I devoted many hours to extracting from her just what she had in mind for the house, and then many more to working up schemes and preparing samples of paint and carpets and dozens of materials. I sent everything over and waited for the verdict.

Silence.

Weeks of silence. Finally, I could no longer contain my curiosity, so I telephoned to ask how she liked my ideas.

"Oh everything is *divine*," she said gaily. "Do forgive me for not asking you to come and see it now that everything is done."

"Done?" I asked.

"Yes," she said. "I took all your wonderful colors and materials to a little shop on Lexington Avenue. I explained just how you wanted everything to look. The man was very clever and bought all the materials at wholesale—the bill was only ten per cent above cost!" The woman was so delighted with herself that I could not speak for amazement.

"I'm so grateful to you," she said. "What taste you have!"

Well, I thought, hanging up rather gently, at least she's honest.

Woman of the Year

A soft voice elocuted into the telephone: I was, was I not, *the* Billy Baldwin who had been with Ruby Ross Wood?

It was a long-distance call from Los Angeles, but the voice said never mind, "Expense Is No Object." We talked endlessly and in great detail about the house the woman and her husband were building.

"I'll die," she said, "if you don't come out and help us." She offered to pay my air fare (first class, if necessary) and put me up for two nights at the Bel Air Hotel.

I was met at Los Angeles airport by her husband, a muscle man, gone prematurely white, dressed in a too expensive, too young, too tight sport jacket. He took me to the tasteless little house from which they were about to graduate. Ms. X was good-looking and well dressed, in a fashionable, impersonal way, and both of them were bursting with vitamins and self-righteous Moderation. There was no way of telling exactly what line of business they were in, but I had the feeling that their success had been achieved without the aid of scruples, and that their careers had in no way been hampered by the intrusion of imagination or a sense of humor.

"There are a few things about you that worry us a little," said Ms. X. "We have heard you are a Southerner, and that you have worked for Jackie Kennedy." I confessed to both crimes with indignant pride. "Also, you are very far away," she continued. "In a job of this Importance it will be necessary for you to spend at least one week a month for the next year with us, and if you have a decent assistant, we would accept his being here another week each month."

"Of course, you understand," interjected Mr. X. reassuringly, "that we are Very Influential People, and Money Is No Object."

Who *were* these people, anyway? I wondered.

"Since you are a Southerner," sighed Ms. X, "we had better tell you right now that our architect is a black man." She mentioned a man whom Mrs. Wood, who had been born in Georgia, used to speak of with uncommon respect. He was, in fact, acknowledged to be a genius, and I told her so.

As if to extricate herself from this uncomfortable development, Ms. X. gestured toward a tiny silver trophy on an abortive coffee table.

"See that silver cup?" she said coyly. "A couple of years ago, I received that cup as Woman of the Year."

"How nice," I said.

Mr. X. apparently did not think I was suitably impressed.

"We represent a lot of people out here," he said. "The Old Guard, the New Guard, the Music World, the Movie World, the Political World, and the Art World." He eyed me challengingly. "Who do you know out here?" he asked.

"Well, not very many people," I admitted. "Cole Porter, George Cukor . . ."

"Oh," scoffed Ms. X., "only the Movie World."

"Of course," remarked Mr. X., "when you come out we won't be able to put you up at the Bel Air—we'll have to find a cheaper place. But tonight, we're going to take you to the most Exclusive and Expensive bistro in town."

"How nice," I said.

The restaurant was mobbed with people. I expected our table to be saluted and overwhelmed by representatives of the Old and New Guards and all those umpteen Worlds my hosts represented. Not a soul so much as acknowledged their presence; but, much to their annoyance, some friends of mine from New York had the audacity to recognize and say hello to *me*.

"Of course, you realize," said Mr. X., "that we are having you thoroughly investigated. We have to know all about your personal life, credit standing, morals, and political affiliations."

"Of course," I said, trying to digest that appetizing remark. "And you realize that naturally I am having you thoroughly investigated, too."

I was enjoying the silence that ensued, when Ms. X., every inch a politician's lady, came to her husband's rescue. "We should tell you that we have already fired one decorator," she said, "although we paid him off Plenty." She mentioned the name of a man I had known for years to be the outstanding decorator of Southern California. I was obviously the luckiest man in the East to have the opportunity to work for these Important People.

The next day, we drove out to see the new Status Symbol. We stopped en route at the old cottage for a moment, where a bovine daughter appeared, thickly made up and dressed dirtily in the hippie clothes of the disenchanted young. I found myself sympathizing with the poor child. At the sight of her, Ms. X.'s expression hardened—from cultivated steel to concrete—and the polish went out of her voice.

"Wash your face and take off those damn eyelashes," she brayed at the girl. "Are you trying to look like Jackie Kennedy?"

The new house was architecturally beautiful—the architect was a man of consummate charm and gentleness.

"I do hope you'll be doing the decoration," he said, but his eyes betrayed him. We walked back and forth through the house for hours, chatting affectionately about Mrs. Wood, having a delightful time in between the remarks and endless questions of the two overfed Egos who marched along with us.

"We would like you to have lunch with us," Ms. X said, drawing me aside, "unless, of course, you won't eat with a black man."

Over Luncheon, she said, "Los Angeles is going to have the finest opera company in the world very soon," as if she were organizing it. "There will be no need for San Francisco to send down its troupe."

I said that I had recently heard a brilliant Tosca in New York, and I mentioned the name of a soprano who has, I think, the most glorious voice on earth—and who also happens to be black.

"Oh," said Ms. X. "But I just can't stand the idea of an Italian tenor in the arms of that black woman."

It was fascinating, I reflected on the plane home, how people could rise to such civic heights. But not fascinating enough to make me want to stay and find out. I telephoned Los Angeles the next day from my office.

"You were right in the first place," I told the Woman of the Year. "We are just too far apart."

CHAPTER 14

Miss G.

IT WAS WINTER. Blustery and bitter cold. I was glad to be home by the fire with two friends in my gardenia-leaf-green living room in Amster Yard. The friends were Julia Welldon, who had one of the most beautiful houses in New York, and Harriette Welles, the charming wife of Sumner Welles. We were having cocktails and chatting merrily, waiting for Cecil Beaton to join us.

Presently, the buzzer sounded, and I went to open the door. My flat was on the second floor, and from my doorway I could see clearly down the stairs to the front door of the building. What came through that door with the rush of icy wind was the most beautiful woman that had ever happened into Amster Yard. The face looking up at me was smiling broadly, framed by an enormous black hat. It was Garbo.

Fur coat flying, she scampered up the stairs and into my living room like a ballet dancer (Cecil rushing along behind her), and pirouetted around the room laughing and sparkling in the firelight. The other two women sat speechless with shock. Suddenly, Garbo became aware of them watching her, and her face hardened from laughter to fright. Like a beautiful silent black moth she ran from the room, down the stairs and out into the winter's night.

Greta Garbo's antisocial nature has not been one bit overstated. She refused to be in the same room with anyone she had not expected to see there. She has never given an autograph in all her life (she carried this policy to such an extreme that, after spending a weekend in the house of one of her most devoted friends, she refused to sign the guest book along with the other guests).

Garbo came to my apartment again a few years later—when it was in its white-and-yellow stage—as one of my guests for lunch on Christmas Day. It had been snowing and it was cold, but the sun was shining brilliantly through the yellow-curtained French windows. As Garbo had been carefully told exactly whom she could expect to meet, I anticipated a pleasant, uneventful afternoon.

She arrived with Allen Porter, of the Museum of Modern Art Film Library. She looked radiant, perfectly at home in the cold, wearing her black fur coat and hat and a simple black wool dress. She handed me her coat and walked straight to the mirror above the fireplace. With a graceful sweep of her hand she caught off her hat, then tossed her head back vigorously, letting her hair fall thick and soft around her face.

Just when we were ready to begin lunch, she went and stood by the long sunny window. "Do you think we could draw the curtains and light the candles?" she asked. Was she joking? Of all the outrageous, spoiled, childish requests, I thought. "Of course!" I said, to conceal my irritation. I shut out my precious New York winter sunshine and proceeded to light all the candles on the mantel, on the table, and in the chandelier. Because of Greta Garbo, we had our caviar and vodka and cold-turkey Christmas lunch by candlelight in the middle of a brilliant Christmas Day.

Garbo stayed practically the whole afternoon. She settled herself in the middle of the sofa, enchanting everyone with her gaiety, her wit, her quick charming laughter, and her repertoire of rather ribald jokes. But even when she appeared most relaxed, she was on her guard. Insistently curious about the private lives of others, she would change the subject if anyone had the effrontery to ask her a personal question.

In the months that followed, I saw Garbo quite a lot, and the next Christmas I invited her to come again for lunch. This time I had fresh candles all ready and was prepared to draw the curtains; it was a dark, dreary day anyway. But, to my astonishment, no request came. I couldn't suppress my curiosity.

"You have just got to tell me," I said, "why you wanted to shut out all that beautiful sun last Christmas, and today, when it's so gloomy . . ."

"You must remember," she answered, "that where I come from there is no sun in winter. When I saw all those pretty candles I thought how nice it would be to have Christmas just as it was when I was a child." What a lovely idea, I thought, hurrying to light the candles, and how happy it would have made everyone the year before if only she had bothered to explain. But then, Garbo never explains.

Although I had known her for more than a year, I did not dare to call her Greta. Almost no one was allowed to call her that. To me, then and forever, she was "Miss G.," and to her, I was "Master Billy."

The better you knew Garbo, the more maddening she became. Occasionally, I would see her on the street. "Hello, Master Billy," she would call. "I never see you." She lived on Fifty-second Street and the river, under the name of Harriet Brown, and absolutely nobody had her telephone number. The only way to get in touch with her was to send a telegram or leave a note.

"Well," I'd say, "why don't you come up for a drink on Wednesday."

"Oh, but I don't know if I'll want to on Wednesday," she'd answer, grinning away at me like a Cheshire cat. Or else total enthusiastic acceptance, and then, five minutes before the appointed hour, the telephone would ring, and it would be Garbo, canceling. Sometimes she wouldn't even call. And as for the idea of inviting you to *her* apartment . . .

One winter it snowed for days and days, making the roads impassable. Children had a field day. The only place to walk was in the middle of the snowbound streets, and that is where I was, on my way home from work in the gun-metal twilight. I turned a corner and, in the pools of light from the street lamps, I thought I recognized a solitary figure bundled in a long fur coat. I hurried to catch up with her and was charmed to see I had been right, for here was Garbo, radiant against the snow, loving it. "I'll walk you home," I offered. We walked along Fifty-second Street, chatting and laughing through the clouds of our breath in the icy air. By the time we reached her building I was so blue with the cold my fingers would not bend at the knuckles. She turned to me, smiling: "How nice of you to come so far out of your way in this biting cold." I hesitated, waiting for the invitation to warm myself before going on, but it never came. She said good night and went sailing in, and I went shivering on my way.

New York had pretty well thawed out when I heard from Miss G. again. Actually, it was George Schlee who called me (he lived with his wife, Valentina, in Garbo's building) to say he was helping Miss G. redecorate her bedroom. They were having some difficulty with the painter, who just couldn't seem to get the color right. Would I help?

I asked my assistant, Edward Zajac, a decorator well known today, to come along —and he was practically overcome with excitement. I told him just to be calm, and gave him as part of his assignment the job of memorizing the number from one of Garbo's telephones. If I was to be running back and forth supervising workmen, her number would be indispensable.

Miss G. opened the door herself, dressed in denim jeans and a man's pale-pink shirt. She and George Schlee took us through the apartment. The painter waited in the hall.

A large L-shaped living room was filled with sunlight from two long walls of windows facing south and east. All the colors were rosy and warm; there were beautiful curtains of eighteenth-century silk, a Louis XV Savonnerie carpet, the finest quality *Régence* furniture, and wonderful Impressionist paintings. I knew Miss G. spent a lot of time browsing through antique shops. How many times had I seen her on walking tours shopping with the Baron Eric de Rothschild, the two of them making a spectacular couple indeed. Their time had not been wasted, either. Her living room was a delight.

Except for the corner nearest the door. Here it was windowless and rather dark, furnished only with a red damask Louis XV *lit de repos* that had belonged to the former Duchess of Marlborough, Mme Balsan, and a coffee table on which several bottles of vodka were all open and consumed to varying depths. Laughing, Miss G. said, "You can see that *this* is where I live."

I felt a little tug on my sleeve, and Miss G. beckoned me playfully with a crooked finger to follow her. She led me to a room that had been intended as a bedroom (her own bedroom was, of course, the only one in that apartment, since there were never any guests), with three walls lined with closets. With obvious pleasure she slid all the doors back and forth, revealing hundreds of dresses. "Master Billy," she giggled, "I have never worn a single one."

All four of us, with the painter in tow, trooped off to the problem bedroom. As we passed through the hall, Garbo mortified Eddie Zajac by telling him: "There's no point in looking at the telephones—all the numbers have been removed."

The bedroom, which overlooked the East River, was a nice square room, practically empty, waiting for its background. Miss G. picked up a small candle shade of shirred mulberry-colored silk and held it up for us to see. "This shade," she said, "was on a candle in a dining car in Sweden—in the first train I was ever on." Then she lit a candle and held it beneath the shade. Our job was to paint the room the color that resulted from the candlelight shining through the silk! The painter looked desperate.

We set to work. The only way to even attempt it was with many coats of glazing. We experimented for hours by sheer trial and error, covering sample board after sample board before finally coming up with a color that was satisfactory to her. I went back to my office exhausted, promising to check back at Harriet Brown's apartment as the work progressed. But when the painter had finished, it was painfully clear that the hard-won color, when it covered all four walls, was quite a bit too strong—and we had to strip and reglaze the whole thing. Finally, we produced the impossible color of flame through mulberry-pink silk, a feat for which we deserved a Nobel prize.

Miss G., totally delighted, paid her bill in person, in full, in cash. She could have saved some money by paying with a check—who would ever have cashed it? But even a check was no reason to sign her name. The only time I ever saw marks made on paper by Greta Garbo was when I was in the hospital, recovering from pneumonia. Darling Miss G. came to cheer me up, but when she was told I was allowed no visitors, she left me a little bunch of flowers with a note. The envelope, printed in pencil, was addressed to "Master Billy Baldwen," and the note said simply, "Good Morning, G.G."

Garbo is a mystery; that, no one can deny. She is at once cunning and endearing, infuriating and divine. I used to see her often in the late afternoon at a flower shop near my office, charming the young shopman into giving her little bunches of the day's leftover flowers. They couldn't possibly last until morning, but they would serve Miss G.'s purposes that night.

She greatly admired people who worked for a living. More than once she said to me, "Master Billy, you and I know what it means to work hard." Allen Porter told me that she used to ask him to run some of her films in the museum screening room, just for her and him. They would sit together in the empty little theatre, Garbo watching Garbo. As she watched, she would whisper into the air, "Now she's going to cross to the window, and hesitate before she speaks . . . now she'll open the book . . . now she'll sit down, very slowly, knowing they're all watching her. . . ." It was as if Garbo were looking at some other actress, familiar yet somehow a stranger.

The last time I saw Garbo was in 1972. I was invited to have a drink with John Galliher, a man of good humor and great taste, who has very attractive apartments in

New York and London. As I walked into the living room, I saw, seated by the fire with her back to me, my dear Miss G. I walked around to greet her. She tilted her face up at me, smiled that unforgettable Garbo smile, and said in that voice uniquely hers, "Small world . . ."

CHAPTER 15

The Fairy-Tale Bedroom of Mrs. Tobin Clarke

THE FAME OF MRS. TOBIN CLARKE'S WHITE BEDROOM had reached me long before I ever saw it. And I needed to see it only once to know that it was the masterpiece of the great decorator Syrie Maugham.

The house itself, designed by David Adler, was a thing of uncommon beauty. It was built on a hillside in San Mateo, California, in such a way that one had only to climb a single flight of stairs to be on the third floor, where the bedroom was, and on a line with the treetops.

The moment I stepped into the bedroom, I was in a fairy tale, my task to find and awaken the sleeping beauty. It was a very tall room, made even taller and airier by the large white bed whose slender bedposts seemed to reach the ceiling—it looked as if the bars had been taken off a giant bird cage. The room was almost square and had an open, delicate, almost ephemeral quality, enhanced by the dreamy fragrance of white petunias blooming in profusion in the garden below.

Since there was an adjoining dressing room for clothing, the bedroom's only real furniture consisted of the bed, with its white coverlet, a few chairs upholstered in white raw silk and arranged on a sculptured white wool rug, a low upholstered silk stool, and a comfortable large wooden bedside table, stripped and treated with glazed white paint. At the windows hung practically nonexistent curtains of unlined white voile.

The color—and the only pattern—was in the wall covering, a contemporary Swedish rough linen just this side of white, crudely stenciled with a scroll design in quite a strong grass green. Only white flowers were allowed in the room but they were, as in all of Syrie Maugham's rooms, extravagantly everywhere.

It was Syrie Maugham, of course, who made the all-white room her trademark. She worked with such boundless imagination and creativity that everything she touched seemed to spring to life, and her famous white rooms had every bit as much vitality and drama as rooms that were multicolored—and twice the romance. She created variations in white by using together every imaginable texture and shading: rough linen, creamy satin, soft velvet, crisp glazed chintz, plenty of fur and wool—and all in shades, from icy blue-white to the color of skimmed cream to the honeyed tones of bleached wood. She also founded a vogue that, thank heaven, still exists: the white carpet, very often of sheared sheepskin or carved patterns in wool, many of them designed and made for her by Marion H. Dorn. Syrie also had an eye for punctuating with just the right amount of jewel-bright color—coral, perhaps, or emerald—to accent all the whiteness. And there was always, somewhere, the glint of crystal. I remember seeing in New York at a decorator's exhibition a room of hers, all various whites except for the walls, which were hung with deep spinach-green damask. It was a knockout.

Everyone has his "abysmal pit," Syrie used to say, and she was obsessed with hers—her daughter Liza; she was devoted to this child, and showered her with the finest little treats and presents she could afford. But she gave Liza her greatest gift without even realizing it—her superb taste. Liza grew up to become the Lady Glendevon, and now lives a charming life in the country in England. She has always made me wonder if good taste is a trait one carries in one's genes.

I met Syrie Maugham at the beginning of World War II, when she was living in New York. She was so fascinating that I made it my business to get to know her when I got out of the army. She had a face that seemed immune to the aging process, with skin as translucent as moonlight. Her voice was soft and pleasant, in its clipped, very British way. She was a wonderful storyteller, and talked one mile a minute, her wit keeping pace, and I never saw her when there wasn't a little hint of witchery in her eyes.

One afternoon, when I was visiting her ill in bed, she said, "Don't you just adore to smuggle?"—as if she were confessing to a secret passion for strawberry sundaes.

"Well," I said, rather startled, "I don't really think I have ever attempted—I'm sure I'd be afraid to . . ."

"I see absolutely no reason at all," she interrupted, "to travel from one country to another unless you smuggle."

I was trying to recover from this blatant admission of piracy when she directed me from my perch at the foot of her bed to the far corner of the room. "Behind the chair is a piece of rolled-up canvas," she intoned. "Bring it here, will you?"

She unrolled the canvas and spread it flat across the bed. It was a painting, about thirty by forty-eight inches. A landscape of green rolling hills and a blue sea. Two ladies, one in pink, one in blue, with matching parasols, strolling in the foreground. I could hardly believe my eyes: here was a signed Monet. I just stood there, floored.

Syrie leaned back against her blue-white pillows, utterly delighted with herself. "That's my latest," she said.

Syrie Maugham's American masterpiece: Mrs. Tobin Clarke's bedroom. Everything is wonderland white, from the sculptured wool carpet to the bird-cage bed with its tasseled tester. Scrolls stenciled on the white linen walls are brilliant grass green. What you must imagine are the white petunias in the garden below and the heady fragrance that filled this room.

CHAPTER 16

Landmarks in Decorating: Revivals and Innovations, 1947-1973

1949　Black and white:
*a gentleman's brown
living room accented with
bright green and punctuated
with a collection of black-and-
white prints and drawings*

1949　Black and white:
*a pink-walled stair hall
in a country cottage, its
woodwork white, its floor
painted black, with a
striking rug and runner
of black and white*

1949 Black and white: *to pep up a conventional pale-yellow room filled with eighteenth-century furniture, a snappy black-and-white linen sofa*

1949 Black and white: *an all-white contemporary dining room smattered with black polka dots painted on white chintz curtains. On the chairs, black cushions; on a nearby table, jet-black tulips*

1953 Monochrome: *a bedroom in shades of brown from off-white to chocolate, with shoji screens, a linen bed, and a floor of saddle leather studded with brass*

1969 Near Eastern furniture: *Moroccan furniture and panel inlaid with mirror and mother-of-pearl, and a gilded Siamese deer—an Eastern setting for a very Western rider*

1963   Cotton and diamonds: *Tiffany jewelry stores across the country, all done in fresh black-and-white papers and cottons to replace outdated velvet. All the furniture is wrapped willow, all the floors covered in white linen.*

1965 Flowers on flowers: *flowered cotton everywhere, fresh flowers by the armful*

1947 The banquette revived: *for dining, playing cards, chatting with friends. At the same time, we took that forbidden color, orange, and made a lady out of her, here with fresh black-and-white cotton slip covers and curtains.*

1939 All white, flashed with green: *my drawing for the
reception room of the Lenthéric perfume salon on Fifth Avenue*

186

1966 Straw: *on the ceiling, on the floor. Straw-wrapped moldings, straw-colored willow-wrapped bookcase. The Indian cotton bed curtains are hung, à la David Hicks, straight from the ceiling.*

1945 Stenciled gold stars: *on the chintz canopy, bedspread, and curtains, and on white-enameled metal chest of drawers. Walls are lacquered the color of a wet gardenia leaf.*

CHAPTER 17

Nostalgia

THERE WAS A VERY GOOD reason why I was in Lady Mendl's apartment that night, drinking White Ladies and standing on her sofa in my stocking feet.

The evening had begun with a dinner party at Mrs. Benjamin Rogers's apartment-and-studio on West Fifty-seventh Street. The room was very tall, with a great north window, and the walls were filled with many of Mary Rogers's own flower pictures she had exhibited at the prestigious Wildenstein Gallery.

Among the guests was Lady Mendl, the founder of interior decoration in America, who was known professionally as Elsie de Wolfe. She was not young even then, but she was extremely pretty, nevertheless, with quick eyes, pale-blue hair, a brisk manner, and brief white gloves it was rumored she removed only when she ate. She may have been tiny, but she had enormous energy and no inhibitions whatsoever.

"Why don't you take Elsie around and show her my pictures," Mary Rogers suggested. "And don't forget," she added with a twinkle, "that they're all for sale."

Lady Mendl was charmed by the beauty and delicacy of the pictures, many of which had a quality that she said reminded her of France of the eighteenth century, the place and period dearest to her heart. Suddenly, she fastened on a lovely small painting of white roses on a dark-green background. She studied the picture for a few seconds, then released my arm and went prancing over to her hostess.

"I like those white roses, Mary," she announced. "I'll buy them."

Fairly soon after dinner, when everyone else was still going strong, Lady Mendl decided she had to go home. Mary leaned over to whisper in my ear. "It would be awfully polite if you'd go with her," she said.

"Well, how nice, young man," she said when I offered to take her home. Her brow furrowed. "But I want to take my picture with me." I went and took it off the wall for her, and away we went to her suite at the Plaza, which she had decorated at the hotel's request.

The room was typical Elsie de Wolfe comfort and pleasant living, and not a hint of ostentation. The walls were a striking deep green, and there was lots of creamy-white damask upholstery, and many chairs and sofas rather loosely slip-covered in green fern on white, the chintz that was one of her signatures.

It was only about ten thirty when we got to the Plaza, and Elsie's faithful secretary, Miss West, was up.

"West," said Elsie, "let's have a little drink." Instantly, or so it seemed to me, there appeared two of Elsie de Wolfe's renowned White Ladies, a remarkable concoction of gin, Cointreau, and lemon juice that was enough to knock your eye out.

"Now take off your dancing pumps, young man," commanded Lady Mendl, "get up on that sofa, and let's hang my picture." Miss West produced the necessary equipment for this operation, and Lady Mendl barked directions from her perspective across the room. At last the picture was up and I must say those roses never bloomed better than they did against that dark-green wall.

"Well, young man," said Elsie, standing on the floor below me with her hands on her hips, "what's the price of that picture? I'm sure you can tell me, since you're obviously taking a commission." I stepped off the sofa, thinking it might be wiser to continue this conversation from a more dignified position.

"Lady Mendl," I said, "how could you accuse me of such a thing? I have no idea of the price, and I certainly am not involved in the sale in any way. I was at Mary's party for fun, not profit."

Lady Mendl, who, I later learned, never did anything unless she could make money on it, looked at me incredulously.

"You, young man, are a fool," she croaked. "You are a decorator, aren't you? You'll *never* get anywhere in this business."

✿

There was many a weekend in the early thirties, before I came to New York, when you could find me at Mr. and Mrs. Robert Deford's rambling white clapboard house near Towson, Maryland, which they called Folly Farm. We by no means roughed it at Folly Farm; there was luxury aplenty—but it was the luxury of ease and peace and simplicity. Everything that happened seemed to be just the perfect thing, and time stood still.

Even the decoration of the old house, which was done in the most positive, personal way by Dorothea Deford herself, was honest and simple. The walls of the entrance hall were papered with a bold black-and-white damask design; a fire crackled in the fireplace at the slightest hint of a chill; and above the mantel hung a beguiling portrait by Sully of a farm boy, his face lit by a sunbeam filtering through the raveled brim of his straw hat. I remember the white-paneled library, full of books, where tea was served every winter's day. And the drawing room, its walls hung with cotton toile, and a piano painted apple green. (As a rule, I like painted pianos not at all, but at Folly Farm what else would you have but an apple-green piano?) The white dining room was lit entirely by candles. Dark old family portraits hung all around, and a square bay window was curtained with unlined white mohair. In summer, that window was never closed, and the mingled fragrances of box and petunias wafted through from the terraced gardens below.

Best of all, I remember the summer weekends at Folly Farm. First, we would play tennis until we could no longer hold a racquet. When everyone was thoroughly worn out, up we'd climb to the second terrace, to sprawl in wicker chairs or the wonderful old-fashioned hammock stretched under an enormous catalpa tree, whose thickly spreading branches formed a lovely rustling outdoor room.

Here we would have hot tea, served always with little silver-dollar-sized tomato sandwiches dripping with fresh mayonnaise. Often, there would be some particularly close match still going on down on the tennis court, and we would hear in the background that very summery sound of racquets and balls connecting in air. After the tea had revived us, out would come the mint juleps, and there we would sit, sipping and laughing, until Robert Deford decided it was time to change for dinner.

There would always be guests—young artists and musicians, and editors and writers from the *Sunpaper*. After dinner, someone would play the green piano, and a little group would gather around to sing.

No one had the slightest concept of the passing of time. "I believe the night owls are about to hoot," Robert would announce on his way to bed. And, sooner or later, most of the dinner guests would drift away.

The heartiest of us house guests stayed up until almost dawn, talking. We must have exhausted every subject known to mankind on these warm, lingering weekends. When it was still very dark, we would creep down to the pool for a starlit dip *à la Russe*, and then, reluctantly, off to sleep as the rest of the world awakened.

❁

It was a glorious spring day—too glorious to be indoors. So Mrs. Miles White and I sat sipping tea in her lovely walled garden in Baltimore, presided over by two peacocks whose sole mission in life was to perch gracefully on the garden wall, their tails arranged like long trains of iridescence.

Mrs. White was in the process of decorating her house, a beautiful symmetrical brick Georgian pile, built in the style of the old houses of Annapolis. I especially remember the drawing room, a lovely soft green, with curtains the color of buttered toast. Mrs. White was a pioneer in the preservation of eighteenth-century American buildings, and had for years been collecting eighteenth-century furniture and silver.

We were about finished with our tiny tea sandwiches when down the path from the kitchen strutted the butler, clad in plum-colored livery, his handsome face the rich color of sweet chocolate, his tight-curled fluff of hair as white as whipped cream. He was carrying a large silver platter upon which sat an exquisite layer cake glistening with thick chocolate icing. I knew just by looking at it how scrumptious it was going to taste.

But the butler did not bring this gourmand's delight to the tea table. Instead, he placed it in the grass some distance away. Instantly, there was an earsplitting shriek, and the two magnificent peacocks swooped down on the cake, screeching in hideous glee. The birds devoured the entire thing in a matter of minutes, while I watched with fascination and not a little envy. Then, not noticeably grateful for their treat, the peacocks resumed their decorative postures on the wall, as if that undignified display had never occurred at all.

❀

I guess not many people have slept in a museum—at least not on purpose. I did, the weekend Harry du Pont invited me to Winterthur, his museum-house in Wilmington. It was a very warm afternoon, and I was whisked directly to the pool, where the other guests were already assembled, swimming and basking in the sun. I couldn't wait to get in the water. After our swim, a butler and a footman appeared to set up a huge tea table covered edge to edge with the most succulent little sandwiches and cakes. It was all very grand indeed, and so pleasant a summer's afternoon that we all just sat around talking until someone noticed it was getting dark. We dressed and went to the house.

I had never seen Winterthur before and it had been invisible from the pool. As I walked toward it in the twilight, it looked as tall as the trees. The butler took me by elevator to the Brandywine Room, where I was to stay. The window- and bed-curtains were made of blue-and-white resist linen, and the room was furnished, like every room at Winterthur, with the finest examples of early Americana. Even then, the house was on public display; so whenever a guest occupied a room, a little gooseneck lamp was brought in to provide reading light, since the room was otherwise lighted, true to its period, only by candles. I had an ample closet and a perfectly modern bathroom with every convenience—nothing old-fashioned here but the charm.

Almost the instant I was dressed for dinner, there was a knock at my door. It was the footman, come to take me down to the great square living room for cocktails of a superior native applejack. This room was papered in a marvelous antique Chinese wallpaper, and in the center of the ceiling hung a blazing mass of crystal, its wonderful soft candlelike light making powdery shadows all around.

We went in to dinner to a table completely furnished with gold-and-white Lowestoft, with a tiny candle flickering at each place. All the men were in black tie, and the ladies were festooned with their most dazzling jewels. But, delicious as they all looked, my fondest memory of that meal was a culinary one: the cream of crab soup, the mere recollection of which is enough to bring tears of pleasure to my eyes.

After dinner, we all toured the house: room after room of extraordinary

American furniture—from the simplest New England pine to the most elaborately painted Pennsylvanian—each room filled with flowers and wonderfully lit. I noticed that, although everything was arranged in strict obedience to the rules of the period, there was still that basic deep comfort that only a real, caring person living there could bring about.

When the tour was over, everyone went to play cards in the conservatory surrounded by great masses of greenery. And, as if to celebrate the occasion of our delightful visit, a night-blooming cereus suddenly unfolded its huge creamy blossom before our eyes.

❁

The telephone rang. It was my friend Diana Vreeland, *Vogue*'s great editor, inviting me to tea. "Of course I'll come," I said. Tea at Diana's was always a delight.

"By the way," she said, "Isak Dinesen will be here."

I practically went through the floor. Ever since I had read *Out of Africa* (Ruby Ross Wood had left it on my bedside table one weekend in 1938, and I found it nearly impossible to leave my room), I had been in love with that brave woman who lived alone and at peace with the animals. And now I was actually going to meet her.

The day came, a cold afternoon in the early spring, and Diana's glowing red living room was warm and cheerful. We sat together at the round, red-clothed tea table. Diana told me that the Baroness (Isak Dinesen was the nom de plume under which the Baroness Karen Blixen wrote books of Gothic stories as well as her African memoirs) was to be accompanied by her secretary and companion, Clara Svendsen, a sensitive and devoted lady who later wrote a beautiful book about the Baroness's life.

At last the bell rang. She was here.

The Baroness was tiny, her cheeks drawn back in draperies of wrinkles, her face set with the deepest, wisest, saddest black eyes I have ever seen. She wore a black funnel-shaped hat thrust forward on her brow, and a black karacul cape with slits, through which protruded two white skin-covered bones that served as arms. On one shoulder rested a huge sheaf of scarlet gladioli ("like a woodsman carrying logs," Diana whispered later). "For your red room," said the Baroness in her smooth deep voice as she handed her hostess the flowers.

The Baroness was visiting New York for the first time from Denmark and was mightily impressed. There were two specific things she wanted to see before going home: a large modern penthouse, and a very small apartment in an old-fashioned house. As the latter perfectly described my own apartment in Amster Yard, I asked the Baroness if she would like to have lunch there the following Saturday.

Imagine my excitement at the prospect of having my heroine in my own apartment. I invited my partner, Edward Martin, and his wife. Edward is probably the most widely read man I know, and has a memory from which nothing has ever been known to escape. I asked Diana if there was anything I should avoid putting on the menu.

"The Baroness eats practically nothing," said Diana, "but adores champagne. Maybe you could have a few grapes for her." I dutifully stocked up on champagne and decided on a bowl of grapes for the centerpiece.

Saturday was a magical day. It was raining gently when my guests arrived, and the fresh green locust trees in Amster Yard looked just-washed. Great drifts of yellow daffodils were blooming their heads off out in the garden. The room, which was then white and yellow, was filled with a lovely light.

"What would you like to drink?" I asked the Baroness as I reached for the champagne.

"I'd like a milk punch," she said with a grin. Ugh. I knew I had the brandy, but I held my breath as I ran to the refrigerator to see if— Yes, thank goodness, there was some milk!

At the lunch table, the Baroness consumed every morsel of the three courses my French chef had provided. And she touched not a single grape. I made a mental note to bring all this to Diana's attention.

The Baroness and Edward talked incessantly through lunch, she, with her beautiful low voice, recalling her life in Africa, he prompting and encouraging her with questions from his vast memory bank. She had lived, she said, a life of beauty and tragedy with animals and natives for several years. She had shot only in defense when a wild animal attacked her. It was difficult to envision this fragile creature with the gentle manner of the nineteenth century ever holding a rifle in her hands, let alone bringing it to bear on an angry beast.

Toward the end of lunch, the Baroness folded her napkin and settled back in her chair. "Would you like to hear a story?" she asked. She began to tell us a tale of love and jealousy that held us spellbound for hours. I didn't even suggest moving to the living room for fear of upsetting the mood. There was no way of knowing whether her story was true, or whether she was spinning a yarn on the spot. The beautiful lulling voice went on weaving its spell, and the rain pattered its background music on the world outside the windows.

❊

When Mrs. William Woodward, a triplet, a great beauty, and the *grande dame* of New York, decided that she would add a wing to the Baltimore Museum of Art as a memorial to her husband, she asked me to help her with the decoration.

194

"Since you are a Baltimorean," she told me, "I think it only fitting that you should make this your homecoming."

I could see the *Sunpaper* headline already: LOCAL BOY MAKES GOOD. And it was all the more fun because the architect was to be my classmate and friend at Gilman School, Francis Jencks.

The new wing was to house Mr. Woodward's collection of English sporting paintings, and Elsie Woodward wanted it to have the atmosphere of a big room in an English country house. Much of the furniture was to come from her enormous New York town house, which she was in the process of dismantling. It was all large-scale eighteenth-century English mahogany, perfect for the project. There were also quite a few lovely subdued Persian rugs that we knew would look marvelous on the highly polished broad-board floor that Jencks had planned.

We decided to paint the walls a warm buff, a typically Georgian color, trimmed in off-white, with large mahogany double doors. Opposite these doors was an enormous Palladian window that looked out onto a pretty wood. After spending some time researching suitable curtain designs and fabrics, I finally chose a slightly tomatoey red damask that picked up the color of the hunting coats of the riders in the paintings.

One of the most spectacular pieces of furniture was in a small anteroom just outside the main room: a mahogany Chippendale breakfront bookcase that occupied the entire length of one wall. We lit the shelves and filled them with the remarkable collection of silver cups won by the race horses from Mr. Woodward's Bel Air stables.

As the work progressed, Elsie Woodward and I commuted between Baltimore and New York by train. I shall never forget those early gay breakfasts in the dining car on the way down, or the dinners on the way back, both of us giddy with fatigue. No matter how difficult the project became, Mrs. Woodward kept us both in the highest spirits. She was a decorator's delight, confident, happy, full of faith.

❀

The year was 1957, and the debutantes at the country ball were somehow younger and softer-looking than debutantes of today. They had a charming, breathless naïveté, their young men bowed, starched and scrubbed, and they danced in one another's arms to music even their parents could understand.

Mr. and Mrs. William Paley gave the party in a beautiful tent in the Manhasset garden of their house, Kiluna Farm, to introduce his daughter Hilary to their friends.

The tent had stripes of pink and white alternating with stripes of flowers in pinks and yellows, red and blue. The tables were covered with pink cotton cloths, with bowls of fresh garden flowers for centerpieces. Hilary was dressed in blushing pink, and Barbara Paley was unforgettable in taffeta of the palest blue.

There was a full moon that night, primordial and mysterious (for the moon was still a symbol of romance in those days, and untainted by progress and scientific enterprise). For a long, lovely moment, it centered itself exactly above the party tent. Bill Paley came to me smiling like an enchanted boy, pointing up at the opalescent moon.

"Can you get the moon to stay just where it is until the party is over?" he asked.

"If King Canute is on your guest list," I replied, "I'll see what I can do."

❊

Of all the great hostesses I knew in my early days in New York, there was none to surpass Mrs. Nathaniel Bowditch Potter. She was a Bostonian by birth, and she brought that breeding to New York. Mrs. Potter was a tall, striking woman with long gray hair that swung shiningly around her oval face. She dressed in sensuous fabrics and lavish furs, and carried her handsome figure so that everyone sat up and took notice. She was full of wisdom and common sense, and loved to have bright people around her. But no matter how bright they were, or how high up in the world, they always felt it was they who were the privileged ones to be invited to Mrs. Potter's parties. It was known around New York that her apartment was *the* place to go.

To begin with, the apartment was a charming one, with the pleasant, uncontrived quality of a perfect little town house. I am convinced that this was due largely to the wonderful rapport Mrs. Potter had with her decorator, Mrs. Archibald Brown, the head of the great firm of McMillen, Inc. Mrs. Brown turned the original, rather unremarkable dining room into an oval and painted it the color of a coral camellia with white trim and simple taffeta curtains. There were niches with classic white marble figures standing in them. When Mrs. Potter had a dinner for eight, she would use her Oriental Lowestoft china of red and pink and white, including plates for cream of tomato soup because it looked so pretty—and tasted so good. The floor was marble so highly polished it reflected the candlelight like moonlight on still water.

For big parties, the buffet was in the dining room, and little pink-covered tables were scattered about the drawing room and library. Everyone came dressed to the teeth, and, although a buffet is thought of as rather informal, Mrs. Potter's buffets always seemed to look as gala as New Year's Eve. The drawing room was painted in *trompe-l'oeil*, with yellow marbleized panels and moldings and yellow curtains. On the wall hung a drawing of Mrs. Potter by her famous cousin, John Singer Sargent. Black and gold lacquer glinted around the room, and there were plenty of painted Louis XVI chairs, comfortably upholstered. The drawing room was lit almost entirely by candles—some in a set of black-and-gold appliques, others in crystal candelabra, the candles all licorice black. Those black candles made such an impression on me that I cannot so much as look at one today without thinking of Molly Potter.

When that very special woman died, she left a wonderful legacy to her daughter: good taste and uncommon style. This daughter, who became Mrs. Russell Davenport, is today a brilliant decorator, without whom the list of top American decorators would be glaringly incomplete.

❊

ROOMS IN MY MEMORIES

In Paris

I will be grateful forever to Rosamond Bernier, editor of *L'Oeil*, for taking me to see 11 Place des États-Unis, the Paris house of the Vicomte and Vicomtesse de Noailles, a beautiful mélange of every conceivable style and period of furniture and object of art. But everything was arranged with such devotion to the personal that the house could have been used as a lesson in furniture arrangement from which every student or seasoned decorator could profit. Never before had I seen grandeur made so intimate. Never have I since.

The *pièce de résistance*—and the masterpiece of the great French decorator Jean-Michel Frank—was the grand salon. This room was so glorious it brought me literally to a standstill. The walls were entirely covered with squares of tawny parchment, from which doors of burnished bronze glowed like fiery eyes in the head of a lion. The chimneypiece was of mica mosaic; there was a screen and some tables of inlaid straw; and almost all the upholstered furniture was slip-covered with creamy linen.

On the walls hung a great many paintings—by Dali, Bérard, Balthus, Magritte, Tanguy, Masson, Chagall, and even Rubens. I was stunned to find myself in such impressive company in a private house. But to the Noailles it mattered not a bit that these were some of the greatest names in contemporary art. It was more important that every one of the artists was their great personal friend—except Rubens, who would have been, I am sure.

In England

"We're going to tea at Sutton Place," announced Kitty Miller one afternoon while I was staying with the Millers in their country house in Sussex. Sutton Place was the house of the Duke and Duchess of Sutherland.

The drive was pleasant, and the scenery seemed to become more beautiful the nearer we came to the house. At last we found ourselves driving through a great park, with spring-green lawns and hundreds of ancient white rhododendrons that seemed to be competing to see which could bloom the most profusely. Suddenly, at the end of the long drive, we saw the house itself. It was built of pale-pink brick, with terra-cotta mortar. "Isn't it lovely," said Kitty. "It looks like a great pink peony."

We were admitted to the great hall, a room of huge proportions that was nevertheless furnished as a wonderfully comfortable living room. The Duke and Duchess had managed to break the size of the room with a pair of immense Coromandel screens, long as they were magnificent. In front of each screen was a long low table. And on each table was a huge tub filled with heroic-sized branches of rhododendrons from the park. But the great surprise was that the branches had been stripped of all their leaves, and their bare tawniness with enormous clusters of white blossoms rose to fabulous heights—looking almost as if the flowers on those fantastic Oriental screens had sprung to life.

In Italy

On the way back from a hectic shopping tour in London and Paris, I was invited to spend a few days with my friend Mrs. Clive Runnells at the sixteenth-century Villa Capponi, near Florence, which she had rented for the month from Mr. and Mrs. Henry Clifford. I arrived exhausted and was taken directly to Mr. Clifford's own bedroom, which had been prepared for me.

When I walked through the bedroom door, I felt as if I had just bitten off a chunk of Alice's Wonderland mushroom. The scale of the room and everything in it was immense. There was an enormous bed and, in the middle of the room, a huge marble-topped table. When I sat on one of the gigantic chairs, my feet barely scraped the floor. It was not only the scale that was grand, of course. The room was filled with treasures befitting an Italian villa, and was also, thank heaven, blissfully comfortable.

But the room's greatest jewel was the bath adjoining it. This was a very long, proportionately narrow room with dark black-green marble walls against which gleamed creamy-white calla lilies clustered in pots around the tub. The lavatory and mirror were between two big windows, a rather unfortunate placement, as it happened. For it was only with the greatest self-discipline that I managed to shave at all. I much preferred to stand at the window, looking down upon the carefully tended lemon gardens with their boxwood borders, where each early morning the gardeners seemed to go about their business on tiptoe. Then my gaze traveled on down, past the clipped hedge and the terraces falling away bank upon bank, across

the grassy valley to the city of Florence, sparkling in the morning sun, and to the lavender hills of Fiesole, hushed and misty in the distance.

During the visit I met some of the world's most fascinating people, among them Harold Acton and Signora Nicky Mariano, who had lived as Bernard Berenson's companion in his nearby villa. One day, Mary Runnells took me to tea at the Villa Sparta in Fiesole to see Her Majesty Queen Helen, Queen Mother of Rumania. She was a marvelous-looking woman, and no one could have been more charming and hospitable, but there was another quality about her as well. Everywhere that great lady moved, there was an aura of gentleness and peace, as if the very birds of the air knew they were in the presence of royalty. Her sweet serenity was all the more poignant when one thought how much great sorrow she had borne: she had been exiled twice, from two countries she loved with all her heart.

After tea, we walked through the gardens, among the arching cypress trees and clipped, sculptured hedges. The Queen herself had planned those gardens, and worked in them every day. As we approached, the crew of gardeners doffed their hats, beaming smiles of affection and respect. Standing in those romantic gardens, I was suddenly captivated by the predominance of blue around me. The lovely blue flowers that were blooming then, the clear blue Italian sky, and the smiling blue eyes of the Queen and Mary Runnells.

In Santa Barbara

I had known Wright Ludington all my life, and his house in Santa Barbara remained the one thing in America I wanted to see and had not. So I was doubly delighted when he called to ask me to come out for a visit.

Even if I had not known Wright's special magic, I would have felt it in that house. As we walked through the rooms, I could feel the powerful force he exerts on his environment—in the architecture, the decoration, and especially in the pictures and sculpture that fill his world.

"Come," he said. "I'll show you to your room."

He opened the door not to a guest room, but to an art gallery. We entered at one corner and looked down what seemed an endlessly long room—at least sixty feet. The white walls were filled with a fantastic collection of paintings of every period and nation. I stopped at every picture. Suddenly, it occurred to me that there weren't any windows—yet the room was filled with light. I looked up to see an ingenious skylight that extended the room's entire length. No one has ever awakened to such glorious sunlight.

At each end of the room was a four-poster bed with blue-and-white curtains. Each bed had its own table, chest of drawers, books, and a good light for reading. The beds were so remote from one another, and the curtains pulled so cozily around them, that even if you had to share the room, it would be like having the place all to yourself.

Beside my bed was the bath and dressing room, painted brilliant yellow, with an enormous window directly above the tub. From that window I could look down the tawny-grassed valley to the blue Pacific far below.

In Maryland

Pleasant Valley Farm, when it was bought by Harvey Ladew in 1929, was a small unpretentious house in some of the best fox-hunting country in the East. Mr. Ladew restored the house to its original nineteenth-century style, then began adding rooms, all connected by arcaded galleries to the main house. Year by year, like Topsy, the house just grew and grew.

But no matter how large it got the distinct personal expression of its owner's taste was never diluted. Mr. Ladew was a devoted Anglophile: if it was English, it was okay. He was also a fox hunter who had ridden in England with the Devon and Somerset staghounds and was former Master of Foxhounds of Maryland's Elkridge-Harford Hunt—a great part of whose country ran through Pleasant Valley Farm.

The best room in the house was the library, designed and built by James O'Connor in the style of the Adam brothers. It was a peaceful room, situated at the very end of one of the new wings, so that no one ever walked through it to get somewhere else. The room was shaped like an oval, its walls painted white, with a shiny waxed bare floor and floor-to-ceiling bookshelves filled with obviously well read books. Opposite the pine entrance door was a green-and-white marble fireplace, extremely rare, with a carved frieze of foxes and hounds. Along the oval's bow on both sides were splendid arched windows sparingly curtained with olive-green serge.

I remember many happy times at Pleasant Valley Farm with Mr. and Mrs. Wood (Chalmers kept a bungalow nearby to use when he came down to hunt) and Marian Hall, another greatly beloved New York decorator. We would sometimes come to the library to have our breakfast, seated on the dark-brown serge sofa and chairs by the fire; or we would come just to be alone, to sit leafing through books at the huge oval mahogany desk in the center of the room.

Although Mr. Ladew was a New Yorker, he rather fancied himself a born Southern colonel, and loved to surround himself with happy people. Some said that Harvey Ladew was hedonistic, but no one could deny that his guests enjoyed with him some of the happiest days of their lives.

In New York

It is almost axiomatic to say that everything Pauline de Rothschild touches turns to loveliness. And the New York town house she owned years ago when she was Pauline Fairfax Potter was no exception. There were two drawing rooms, one white with gold-leaf moldings; the other an extraordinary color taken from a Hermès umbrella—some people were convinced it was gray, others that it was mauve, and still others that it lay somewhere between brown and green. The furniture and art were beautiful, as one might expect, and all through the house there were the tiny, unexpected human touches that were Pauline's way of making everyone feel welcome and loved. One of these I shall always remember with a smile: Pauline's parade of camellia trees.

Every year they came, about a dozen of them, very tall and covered with blossoms in purest white and every shade of pink. Pauline put them everywhere—in front of the windows, in wide doorways, beside a reading chair, by the bookcase, near a bed, anywhere her myriad guests were likely to be, so they might have this extra gift of loveliness.

CHAPTER 18

Green Mansions

A Garden at Le Clos Fiorentina, the House of Roderick Cameron at St. Jean-Cap Ferrat

To surround his eighteenth-century house in the south of France, Roderick Cameron has designed and planted the most delightful gardens, each with its own special flavor and charm. My favorite is a very small garden sunk deep below the terrace, which is used in summer as a comfortably furnished sitting-dining room with a luxuriant grapevine for a ceiling.

The sunken garden is a simple rectangle divided by box borders into thick beds of white begonias centered with wonderful, silvery-green foliage and twin orange trees in big terra-cotta Florentine pots. Planted at the end of the path: white espaliered lantana. The chiaroscuro of lights and darks is created by a variety of greens that run from that pale silver-dust green to flute notes of piercing emerald.

The garden has no ceiling other than the sky, and is totally surrounded by trees and greenery—an oasis in the midst of nature's ebullience. But for all its style and sophistication, the garden's design is so controlled that it could easily be adapted to a plot the size of a postage stamp. Its almost *trompe-l'oeil* scale makes it seem much bigger than it is. The garden has the quality of a medieval tapestry, only wonderfully fragrant, where noble knights and ladies walk.

The Greenhouse of Mrs. Paul Mellon at "Oak Spring," Upperville, Virginia

The Virginia countryside is covered in silence and snow. You look from the warm house through the garden to the greenhouse. It is a glass pavilion, the central dome of which is crowned by a bronze finial designed and executed by Jean Schlumberger, the twentieth-century Cellini of Paris.

Under the nacreous winter sky, you come to the entrance, which opens into a square room done entirely in cupboards, the doors of which are painted in a *trompe-l'oeil* of garden instruments, baskets, "pinned-up" letters from children and friends, and a poem by Paul Mellon.

To the left and right, long galleries extend. But these are *allées* of flourishing flowers, plants, and trees—mimosa, olive, orange, and lemon. On the floor, which is laid in old bricks in eighteenth-century parquet designs, sit the little herb trees—rosemary, thyme, myrtle, silvery santolina—clipped and neat and proud. Along the borders bloom South African annuals and eighteenth-century bulbs from Holland.

The special greenhouse aroma is here punctuated by the citrus blossoms and the jasmine that "papers" the white bricks. Other walls are espaliered with Chinese lacquer-red nasturtiums on bamboo frames.

Above all other sensations, smells are the most nostalgic; here, every pleasure of a lifetime is recalled, through the horticultural genius and imagination of Bunny Mellon.

My favorite of Mr. Cameron's gardens at Le Clos Fiorentina

*Mrs. Mellon's greenhouse
in Virginia, a summer
garden even when
surrounded with snow*

205

An Arabian Night: The Metropolitan Museum of Art Centennial Ball, April 13, 1970

WHEN THE DIRECTORS of the Metropolitan Museum of Art asked me in February of 1970 to help them with their one hundredth anniversary celebration that April, I accepted with enthusiasm. After all, how many chances does one get to decorate a great museum? There were to be four ballrooms, and I was to share the decoration with three other firms: Burge-Donghia, Parish-Hadley, and McMillen, Inc.

My assignment was to transform the Fountain Restaurant, an enormous lunchroom for museumgoers, with a reflecting pool running its length, into a crowded 1970's-style discothèque, open for dancing from midnight until dawn. How, I asked myself, was I supposed to create, in the space of less than two months, an intimate, smokily lit, hard-rock discothèque in a room as vast as the Sahara? And, as if that were not challenge enough, I was informed that since the Fountain Restaurant was open every day, I would not be able to take over the room until the very eve of the ball. This meant that, although everything would be designed, measured, and prepared in the weeks beforehand, it all had to be installed in less than twenty-four hours. The first thing I did was recruit my talented associate Arthur Smith, but I was convinced that the task I had undertaken would require several hundred elves as well.

A ballroom has to be strong, grand-scale, dramatic—no fine little details here, no pretty bouquets. It must be larger than life and have the impact of the theatre. We contracted genuine theatre craftsmen to help us.

Somehow, we had to get rid of the pool and at least some of that vast empty space. We decided to build a room within the room, using nothing but fabric. We needed hundreds and hundreds of yards, to be draped on huge wooden frames from ceiling to floor. I already knew just the perfect fabrics; the question was, Could we get them in time? They were fantastic cotton prints inspired by the *art nouveau* paintings of Klimt. Woodson Wallpapers was only just beginning to print them, but I got my good friend Woodson Taulbee to agree to do a special printing just for the ball. We chose a particularly strong pattern, some yardage in red, some in blue, for the predominant background, and other, smaller-scaled prints to go with it. In every one of them, metallic gold paint glimmered richly.

The tables, I felt, should be quite empty, simply covered to the floor in red-and-blue cotton cloths. Instead of flowers, there would be palm trees. And something would have to be done with the tremendous white iron chandeliers—each taller than a man—that hung like giant teardrop bird cages from the ceiling: we decided to make enormous slip covers that looked like harem pants. The room was shaping up into a sexy Middle Eastern sultan's tent.

The Fountain Restaurant at the Metropolitan Museum of Art as it looked before we waved the magic wand. Its feeling of austerity and expansive space, the openwork chandeliers, and the central pool made it very unlike a discothèque. Opposite: The same room on the night of the ball. We blocked out the pool, slip-covered those chandeliers, and erected walls—all with the same splendid cotton—and succeeded in creating an intimate magic-carpet world.

208

By the appointed hour, we had prepared everything as far as possible. Then the theatre craftsmen arrived, and we were in business. We worked all day hammering frames together, affixing fabric, erecting, draping, fitting, adjusting, securing—all with the help of the agreeable museum staff (the elves I had prayed for), who spread the tables and prepared the serving areas. We held our breath as the huge empty fabric balloons were slipped over the lights. They had to be perfect; there were no second chances. They fit snugly and looked marvelous.

At the same time, three other worlds, each completely distinct, were being created in other parts of the museum. The building fairly rocked with activity. We were greatly tempted to go see what the other decorators were doing, but we forced ourselves to wait and be surprised.

By late afternoon, we were ready to have our first lighting rehearsal. The effect was glorious; the room was filled with smiles of satisfaction. We gathered our tools and supplies, swept up, and went home to change for the party.

When we returned a few hours later, the Metropolitan Museum was transformed. In the blackness of the New York night, the building was ablaze with light and filled with the most dazzling array of people ever assembled for a single event. There was a brilliant cross-section: wealthy dowagers dressed to the teeth, Beautiful People, celebrities from the theatre, motion pictures, music, art, and literature, the ubiquitous politicians, luminaries of the social world, and marvelous-looking young people dressed in the most far-out costumes one could imagine. The merry throngs proceeded to the various ballrooms along broad strips of red carpeting. The greatest party New York has ever seen was under way.

The first ballroom was the evening's masterpiece: a fantastic adaptation of a 1930's roof-garden supper club, created by Angelo Donghia in the Egyptian sculpture gallery. Towered over by eight huge stone sphinxes—permanent museum residents—the room sparkled with silver-lamé draperies, illuminated turquoise columns, a ceiling of colored glass, and everywhere masses of orchids—all bathed in lighting that had the quality of moonlight. I consider it the best ballroom decoration I have ever seen. In this sumptuous setting, the guests had their cocktails and canapés, and danced to a band led by Meyer Davis himself.

Dinner was served in the second ballroom, the central armor gallery, which Parish-Hadley had turned into a lovely romantic setting of the 1870's. Everything was gilt and white; the room was filled with bouquets the size of trees, and overflowed with lilacs and lilies and all the flowers of spring. A twenty-two-piece string orchestra struck up the waltzes, and the fare was oysters, champagne, and pheasant pie.

The museum's Blumenthal patio was transformed by McMillen, Inc., into a ravishing *Belle Époque* background for dessert and coffee. The tables were clothed in pink and cerise and centered with wreaths of flowers and flickering cathedral candles.

Palm trees, banana trees, and hundreds and hundreds of pink cinerarias filled the room; tucked into every available niche were lovely little Turkish corners, all done in saccharine confectionery pinks. The triple-tiered buffet tables, like great pink wedding cakes, were crammed with ices, pastries, lovely cups of strawberries, and pink champagne.

None of the three rooms was ever too crowded or too empty—the great fun of the party was that every one of the two thousand guests could move freely from ballroom to ballroom. Nor was the ball limited to the ballrooms. The museum itself had undergone an extraordinary transformation and was showing off its fresh new face almost for the first time that evening. The immense entrance hall, once dingy and rather drab, had been scrubbed from top to toe, revealing its splendid architectural detail in its full glory. All the galleries had been repainted and the art rehung; the galleries and the broad connecting corridors were all wonderfully lit. This was also the first appearance of the great continuing gift of Mrs. William Wallace: huge bouquets of fresh flowers in tall stone niches around the entrance hall. The flow from room to room among the fantastic treasures was now so easy that you could just walk tirelessly on forever. Drifting back and forth at the ball, you would meet people unexpectedly, taste the wines and sweets, sit and talk for a while at a pretty table, and maybe dance with a star.

Two hours later, after the glamour of the three dining ballrooms, all the guests took the long trip, on a very long red carpet, to the south end of the museum and into the hectic atmosphere of my 1970's disco. There they had a huge buffet of omelets and crepes, coffee and doughnuts, created right before their eyes. There was an earsplitting rock band with a beat that reverberated to the very soles of the feet, and was reinforced by records and tapes. And absolutely none of it let up until dawn.

Everyone had told me to expect to see my room less crowded than the others because by midnight all the old folks would have taken themselves home to bed. Well, they certainly did not. My room was packed, and if the young people did most of the dancing, their elders watched and listened with delighted fascination, stuffing themselves with fresh doughnuts. The disco was still swinging at five in the morning. The museum people had to resort to putting the lights out to get the guests—and the band, too—to go home.

By noon, museumgoers were relaxing quietly in the vast Fountain Restaurant, having lunch, watching the reflections in the placid pool. The music and the doughnuts were gone; the white iron chandeliers stood once again quite naked; the palm trees, the giant scaffolding, the twelve hundred yards of gold-struck fabric had all disappeared, as if by magic. There was not a scrap of evidence that only a few hours before, in this room, in this building, had been created a magical Arabian night —a night of wonder that can occur only once in a hundred years.

CHAPTER 20

A House in the Country, 1974

SURROUNDED BY GENTLY ROLLING WOODLAND so thick that even in winter all you can see of your nearest neighbor is the curling smoke from his fire, there stands a house that to me is the essence of country life. It is just an hour's drive from the metropolitan bustle, but its atmosphere is perfect for the children, horses, and other living things that are growing there.

The minute the owners saw the house they fell in love with it. The original house was built by Francis W. Roudeush in 1954, and the children's wing added by James Leslie in 1958. It is a simple, straightforward frame structure of decidedly New England flavor, with a room for each child and the nurse, a fireplace in every room, a broad rear terrace that overlooks a lawn and pool, and, most important, a lot of woods filled with secrets for curious children to discover.

The house did need a bit of letting out at the seams, however, since it had one glaring omission: a master bedroom. The owners decided to add a new wing with an upstairs bedroom. They wanted the wing to be at once contemporary and in sympathy with the existing achitecture. I told them Jack Coble, who built Cole Porter's library-bedroom wing in Williamstown, was the man for the job.

Jack Coble's plan gave them not only the second-story bedroom they wanted, but also a lovely downstairs sitting room as well. Not that they needed a sitting room; but *something* had to hold up the bedroom. Besides, the new room would catch a lot of pleasant light, as well as the overflow of books from the well-stacked library next door. Jack also arranged for a little hallway downstairs and a dressing room above. Everyone was delighted. Then it was my turn.

The outside of the old house was a proper but rather boring taupey color, so the first thing we did was paint the whole thing a delectably daring pumpkin—paled down, but not much. The perfect color, we thought, for a house whose name is Thanksgiving. All the trim is creamy white, including the coins—those big wooden reinforcement blocks at each corner. The front door, set out from the house by a little glass enclosure, became a shiny dark-brown exclamation point.

This door opens into a wonderful big room of the sort known in England as a living hall because it is used as both a living room and entrance hall. There is a lovely low farmhouse quality about the room, with its fireplace, white-banistered staircase leading gracefully off to the left, and banks of French doors opening onto the terrace. The floors are beautiful polished dark wood, full of reflections, and only partly covered by a brown-and-white Moroccan rug. The walls we painted pure white.

The furniture in the house had belonged to my clients for years; we discovered with gratitude and pleasure that it would all fit, and would need only to be re-covered.

In the living hall, we made most of it country brown and white: two big squashy sofas by the hearth are covered in shiny brown chintz diamond quilted with natural wool thread; a couple of French chairs are upholstered in beige leather; a settee by the staircase is done in a pretty brown-and-white-striped linen; and at the windows a brass card table has a top slip-covered in cream-colored suède. We just couldn't keep all that delicious pumpkin outside, so it appears—in cotton and undiluted this time—on a big upholstered chair by the fire, a wood-framed settee across the room, and in curtains smartly trimmed with brown-and-white braid.

All the pictures are very personal indeed, especially the two romantic old family portraits, still lovingly hung in their original rather elaborate gilt frames.

To the right of the living hall is the dining room, small, charming, full of light, with a lovely fireplace. The furniture consists of an English mahogany pedestal table placed windowward of center, eight white-lacquered Chippendale chairs, a Queen Anne tortoise-shell mirror over the fireplace, and quite an eccentric mahogany sideboard with drawers from the floor up. We created a sunny background in one sunny stroke: wallpaper and matching cotton curtains of chamois yellow, printed with fresh white ferns.

To the left of the living hall, a small straw-carpeted passageway and a little brown-lacquered bar lead to the square library, also carpeted with straw. Here the walls are painted dark shiny brown—a fact difficult to discover, since they are entirely book-lined. Large French doors give onto the terrace; a couple of smaller windows are curtained in unlined cream-colored glazed chintz—luminous with the sunlight coming through. Furnishings are ample and comfortable: a large desk, an English drum table loaded with photographs, a fine eighteenth-century tub chair in fawn-colored suède. The excitement of the room is the slip-cover fabric on the sofa and chairs: outrageous black-and-white tulips on a pale honey-colored cotton—a recoloration of an old document.

The next step you take is up—to the new wing. By way of the little white hallway, full of pictures and a nice old English chest, you come to the new sitting room.

Where this room isn't glass, it's white. White walls and bleached wood floors; the big windows onto the terrace draw-curtained for glare with white voile; simple white duck Roman shades for the three smaller windows. Already there is a whole wall of overflow books from the library, and the television is here, too: it is a very family kind of room.

The main seating group backs up to the bookcase: a big beige linen sofa and four enormous fat armless chairs covered with sensational black-brown-white floral on a background of cobalt blue so pure it might have just been squeezed from the tube. The coffee table, a giant to serve the needs of all sitters, is of beige leather. Near one window stands a French Provincial *refraichessoir*, a piece of furniture originally meant to hold wine bottles, but which modern man has ingeniously put to use for potted plants.

The master bedroom, which is what the new wing is all about, is reached, like the children's rooms, via the living-hall staircase. The room is tall, with a wonderful contemporary cathedral ceiling painted gleaming white. Yet there is a soft enveloping feeling, as if the whole room were made from an eiderdown quilt. We painted the walls the softest corally camellia color, trimmed with white, and the perfectly enormous bed is spread with linen of the same lovely color, but with a little more depth. I designed the headboard and bedside tables—all wrapped wicker, the tables topped with white formica. Rather handsome, I think. The pinky-beige rug is woven raffia—could a bare foot ask for anything more heavenly?

The curtains (white voile) and shades (white duck) are exactly like the ones in the sitting room downstairs—thoughtfully planned to create a handsome balanced façade for visitors approaching the pumpkin shell.

The library in the original part of the house

The master bedroom, above, *upstairs in the new wing.* Right: *the sitting room in Thanksgiving's new wing. The original house,* opposite, left, *was built in 1954. Children's wing was added in 1958, bedroom wing in 1973.* Opposite, right: *the house as it looks from the garden.* Opposite, below: *the living hall*

CHAPTER 21

Apartment in the Sky: Mr. and Mrs. Harding Lawrence, 1973

THIS IS AN EXTRAORDINARY APARTMENT—a triplex hung over a river—for an extraordinary family. The Lawrences have owned the top two floors for several years, and when that inevitable time came for the children to embark on busy social schedules of their own, the floor below was acquired as well. The building is handsome but rather old-fashioned: it took the brilliant architect Page Cross nearly a year to get the apartment working the way the owners wanted it.

The most obvious major change was the installation of a glass wall in the living room and broad floor-to-ceiling windows in all the river-view rooms of the two upper stories. What better way for city-bred children and their parents to spread their wings than a skyscraping perch where the visibility is, on a clear day, forever? Before the advent of the new glass wall, the living room was a rather dim, narrow tunnel. Now it stretches right to the edge of the surrounding terrace. The owners wanted colors that would keep the room in the sky; so, of course, it is blue and white, which is what the heavens are made of. To give the room a solid footing on a cloud, I paved the floor with squares of white vinyl, then found the clue to the whole decorating scheme, a ravishing blue-and-white antique Indian durrie rug for a magical Tunisian look.

I was going mad trying to find exactly the right furniture for my magic-carpet room, so I designed it myself: banquettes and chairs with Turkish pantaloon skirts. The blue chair covering is rough raw silk, a sort of regal denim. The banquettes are covered with the wall fabric, a creamy grège textured cotton, nice to touch. The pillows look like silk brocade but they aren't. They're cotton and linen.

We already had the immensely decorative Indian-wood and ivory mirror to hang over the fireplace, but I was desperate about the mantel. Some conventional French thing just wouldn't do. I asked one of my partners, Arthur Smith, to design a mantel, and he came up with a perfect one—polished steel and mirror. Now, I thought, what this room needs is something eccentric, something astounding. By sheer luck, I found it: a pair of tall painted-wood Mogul finials carved as intricately as lace—finials as old, maybe, as Akbar. The result is perfection: the great new, the great old.

To widen the room, we grouped all the furniture on the fireplace wall. On paper, the floor plan looked rather lopsided, but in reality it is perfectly balanced—another proof of the eye's unfailing logic. The opposite wall of glass is almost unfurnished, except for a substantial contemporary table of polished steel and Lucite, on which rest some precious objects, including a fantastic full-head African mask made of animal hides and encrusted with beadwork.

The huge painting is by Pousette-Dart, who also did two smaller ones on the

The sky-hung living room, filled with the greatest of the old, the best of the new

opposite wall. The lovely rosy wash is by Helen Frankenthaler, and the nude, one of Mr. Lawrence's favorite pictures, is by Milton Avery.

In a sensible way, the owners are unabashedly sensuous. They love to be comfortable after a long working day; color that delights and revives; delicious things to eat and drink; privacy, but with air and light and sunshine; and time to spend with their children, the joy and fascination of their lives. All this means that architecturally the apartment must work not only hard but smoothly. Storage and clothes closets and even little rooms for laundry and the preparation of food are tucked strategically all through the apartment, concealed and made invisible behind flush doors covered with the same vinyl as the corridor walls. The lighting is perfect, with sources recessed in ceilings, and everything that should be is bathed in light.

A short hall, off which is a powder room in dramatic brown and white, extends from the living room to the dining room, all of which is paved in white vinyl. The dining-room floor is spread with a twin of the blue-and-white durrie rug (imagine, if you can, the miracle of finding two!). As a rule, dinner is served at the corner banquette, on the round table swathed in blue silk. The white-lacquered Venetian chairs have brown leather seats. For larger gatherings, another table and lots more chairs are set up near the window. That big painting is seventeenth-century Dutch. Walls are hung with the same cotton as the living room, nonstop.

Dining is by no means limited to the dining room. The Lawrences like to eat literally all over the place, and their pleasure is easily catered to by those kitchens and pantries within reach of everywhere. On cold winter nights, with that high-altitude wind howling and the snow coming down like ticker-tape, there's nothing snugger than dining, as they often do, at a table simply drawn up in front of the fire.

You descend—via a handsome open brass-railed stair hall decorated with a huge, smashing Helen Frankenthaler—to the second floor. Here, with curtains and Roman shades pulled out of sight, the rooms have the openness of a stage with its curtain up, and the light streams in as though it came from sky-hung klieg lights. The entire floor is devoted to the personal comforts of the family. They were very definite about how things should work; how they looked was pretty much up to me. Nothing inspires a decorator as much as the implicit trust of his clients, especially those whose taste he knows and respects. In the master bedroom I had a field day. It is a ravishing room, mainly because of the colors—one shade of apricot after another: palest for walls; in velvet on the French chairs and superplump chaise longue; in *chinoiserie* chintz on the other chairs and curtains; and in a silk-hung bed to end all beds. The bed curtains

The top-floor dining room

*The family room on
the lowest floor*

draw, pleasant on a winter's night—the Lawrences have developed the habit of drawing the bed curtains rather than the ones at the huge windows—and there's lighting inside to read by. It's almost like a little house. And there is some black lacquer furniture for punctuation.

The first stop after the bedroom is Mary Lawrence's bath, which is dazzling. She asked for mirrored walls, and got a mirrored ceiling, too. She says it's good for her figure. Since the only passers-by are birds, she bathes in full view of the elements; lying back in her tub, she can look up in the mirrored ceiling and watch reflections of barges on the river and the traffic roaring fourteen floors below. Her dressing room is next door, and, since closet doors would have been cumbersome, it is entirely curtained in the bedroom chintz and lighted to perfection.

Opening from her bathroom is Harding's, where walls and ceiling are sheathed in black glass that looks exactly like burnished onyx. He hasn't been in a tub for years, and the usual ritual is to hop from the shower to his dressing room-study, where he likes to pull the Roman shades to the ceiling and lie in the sun on a long chaise I had made to measure for him. It doesn't matter how damp he is—the nylon suède covering is velvety, but waterproof and cleanable as oilcloth.

The study-dressing room, carpeted with a tawny spotted thing that looks like antelope, is where the Lawrences often come for cocktails or even a midnight snack. It's only when the curtains that hang all around the walls are pulled back that you realize they mask an arsenal of storage space for every kind of clothing a man is ever likely to acquire. The fabric is a French chintz with enough color in it to keep the apricot of the bedroom going from one end of the suite to the other. Each room has its own character, but there are no violent jumps.

Since the lowest floor is leased, not owned, no architectural changes were permitted. No one minded at all.

The little airy room where guests are sometimes given a cocktail is called, simply, the sunroom. The chintz has an old Japanese motif; the colors are from nature: straw on the floor, lots of browns and basket tones and greenery. The black-and-white drawings are by Al Held, and Ward Bennett designed the terrific woven-wicker sled chairs.

Off the sunroom is a room that is part music room, part library, part sitting room. The term family room isn't fashionable any more, and what a pity. Our Colonial ancestors used it, and it fits this room exactly. The original paneling was awfully woody, so we lacquered it the color of a wet brown seal, and the glazed chintz Roman shades are the same color. However, it is anything but a sobersides room. The rug is a prettily faded Aubusson; the linen velour sofa and chairs are outrageously comfortable; and there is provision for any activity a family can enjoy together. The abstract over the black chesterfield sofa is by Okada, beautiful and delicate. The Frankenthaler above the mantel is like a pennant caught gaily in the wind.

The sunroom, looking into the family room next door

*Mr. Lawrence's dressing room,
with closet curtains open, above,
and shut*

The master bedroom. Opposite: *Mrs. Lawrence's scintillating mirrored bath.*

Index

Figures in italics indicate pages on which pictures occur.

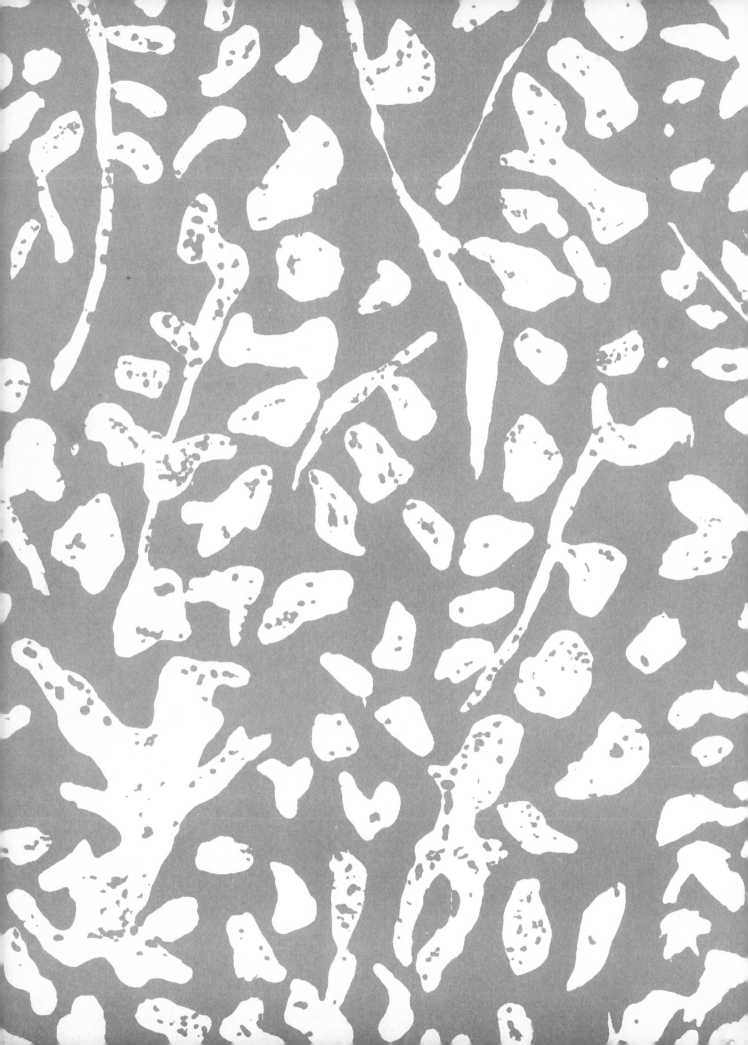